D1627183

This book is being distributed courtesy of
The Southwest Regional Center
for Drug-Free Schools and Communities
A Division of Continuing Education and Public Service
The University of Oklahoma
555 Constitution Avenue, Suite 138
Norman, Oklahoma 73037
Telephone: (800) 234-7972 (out of state),
(405) 325-1454 (in Oklahoma)

WILLIAM A. LOFQUIST

DISCOVERING THE MEANING OF PREVENTION

A Practical Approach To Positive Change

 AYD PUBLICATIONS

ASSOCIATES FOR YOUTH DEVELOPMENT, INC.
P.O. BOX 36748, TUCSON, ARIZONA 85740

DISCOVERING THE MEANING OF PREVENTION
A Practical Approach To Positive Change

For information contact: Associates for Youth Development, Inc.
P.O. Box 36748
Tucson, Arizona 85740
Telephone: (602) 297-1056

Library of Congress Catalog Card Number – 83-72268

The quotation from *Developing Attitude Toward Learning,* by Robert F. Mager, copyright 1968 by Pitman Learning, Inc., reprinted by permission of Pitman Learning, Inc.

The quotation from *The Aquarian Conspiracy: Personal and Social Transformation for the 1980s,* copyright 1980 by Marilyn Ferguson, reprinted by permission of J.P. Tarcher, Inc., Houghton Mifflin Company.

Portions of the first draft of this book were completed under grant number 78-JN-AX-0100 from the National Institute of Juvenile Justice and Delinquency Prevention of the U.S. Department of Justice. The contents do not necessarily reflect the views and policies of this grantor agency.

Book and cover design by JoAnn Alwin. Type set by Sunrise Graphics, Inc.

ISBN 0-913951-00-5

Printed in the United States of America

First Printing August, 1983
Second Printing October, 1985
Third Printing August, 1989
Fourth Printing February, 1991

This book is dedicated to my parents,
Kathryn and Henry Lofquist;
and to Mary, Laura, Peter, Ellen and Mike
– a community of people who daily
promote my well-being.

contents

Foreword, Kenneth Polk, Ph.D. – iii
Preface – vi
Acknowledgements – viii

Chapter I –
What Does "Prevention" Mean? 1
Definitions of Key Words – 2
Arenas of Human Service Activity: Putting
    Prevention in Context – 4
Common Attitudes About Prevention – 13
Actively Fostering Prevention Capacity – 15

Chapter II –
Basic Ideas for Building Prevention Capacity 17
A Validity Test for Workable Prevention Strategies – 18
Some Positive Values Undergirding Prevention Activity – 19
The Essential Elements of a Change Process – 20
Some Basic Assumptions for Prevention – 23
Focusing on Conditions – 25
Identifying the Skills Needed for Prevention – 26
Engaging Key Allies for Prevention – 30
A Practical Strategy – Small Group Action Training – 32
Three Stages of a Well Designed Prevention Initiative – 33
Some Rules-of-thumb for Developing Prevention Strategies – 35

Chapter III –
The Economics and Politics of Prevention 37
Organizational Lifestyles and Prevention – 39
Forces That Shape Human Services – 44
Does Your Community Have a Well-defined
    Prevention Policy? – 51
Conducting a Community Prevention Inventory – 55

Chapter IV –
Viewing the Community from a Prevention Perspective . . . 57
The Youth Opportunity Planning Process
    (Parts I and II) – 59
Common Conditions Affecting People in Most Communities – 72
Using a Prevention Perspective – 77
Occasions for Action – 79

Chapter V –
Planning for Action. 85
First Steps Towards Planned Change – 86
The Prevention Formula – 89
The Project Worksheet – 97
Force Field Analysis – 99
The Youth Opportunity Planning Process (Part III) – 101
Avenues for Broad Citizen Involvement – 103
Maintaining Community Support – 105
Following Through to Achieve Results – 106

Chapter VI –
Gauging Your Progress 107
Why Gauge Progress? – 108
The Key to Gauging Progress Is Good Planning – 112
Five Evaluation Levels for Gauging Progress – 114
Determining the Quality of Efforts to Gauge Progress – 119
Designing a Monitoring Program for Community
Development – 121

Chapter VII –
Building a Support System for Prevention 123
Prevention As a Group Task – 125
Advocacy and Technical Assistance: Twin Forces for
Positive Change – 128
Developing Local and Statewide Prevention Networks – 132
The Statewide Positive Youth Development Initiative – 138
The Challenge of Being Proactive in a Reactive World – 145
Achieving a Balance in Human Service Resources – 146

Footnotes 149

Annotated Bibliography. 150

foreword

Kenneth Polk, Ph.D.

This is an important and timely work. It is important because it concerns what continues to be a major challenge throughout the developed world: how to prevent such problems as juvenile delinquency, drug and alcohol abuse and many other symptoms experienced by young people. It is timely because it throws a most needed ray of light on the issue of how communities might themselves take action at a time when we suffer from a lack of leadership and intellectual bankruptcy at national and state levels. A typical result of the major policies currently being promoted in political arenas is prison overcrowding, which has reached crisis proportions. Surely we are ready for better alternatives. This book is a step in the right direction. Its significance would seem to rest on the following factors.

One, it is written so that it provides a clear statement of what is meant by prevention. Nothing has more hampered an understanding of prevention policies than the fog of confusion about what the term means. Virtually anything might be, and probably has been, proposed to prevent youth problems. In the past few years, it has been argued that such things as more boxing gloves, selling newspapers, and even walking dogs, are prevention activities. All are perhaps justifiable on some grounds, but their direct impact on the problem is hard to demonstrate. This book clearly outlines the community development approach and shows how it differs from other approaches, such as remediation.

Two, this work makes clear that prevention has political elements. What is identified and delineated is a process of community change based in an explicit and practical political framework. All too often writings about prevention concern themselves with substantive features of programs, perhaps grounded in specific theories, with little or no reference to the needed processes of community decision making that must take place if the programs are to be implemented. Here the reader will find a concise statement of how one can initiate and participate in a process of community change that will lead to positive youth development.

Three, the forms of community change identified are those which vest a sense of ownership of local residents in the forms of youth development that result. This is a book about community participation. It specifies that the ultimate responsibility for change will be in local hands, an approach which is in sharp contrast to the pessimism of the policy makers who continue to build large, coercive state and federal institutions as a solution to many youth problems. Among the many destructive features of institutional solutions is the fact that they remove any sense on the part of the community that it is responsible for either the problem or its solution.

iii

Four, the view of community change that emerges from this book is one that emphasizes small-scale starting points. The process identified is one that individuals can do. Inherent in the point of view here is that the discussion presented should give individuals a step-by-step set of procedures which they can follow to initiate programs of prevention. This is not an abstract analysis which leaves the practical implications for others to fill in. Yet it is theoretical in that the reader will certainly be left with some sense of the political and economic parameters within which the community effort must function. It avoids stating these in such a way that the problem of youthful trouble seems either too large or too complex for individual persons in individual communities to tackle.

Five, an emphasis is given in this discussion to the specification of measurable results as part of the process of prevention. All too often, prevention programs suffer from confusion about what is to be achieved. What is absolutely essential for professionally defensible prevention efforts is clarity both about outcomes and the procedures necessary to achieve these outcomes. Emphasizing the importance of an explicit statement of measurable results makes it possible for others later to follow and understand both what was attempted and why. For the individuals conducting the prevention program, the specification of outcomes in measurable terms provides clear targets that the efforts are aimed toward; these targets serve as constant compass headings regarding where the program is going.

Six, this book underscores the importance of evaluation as part of the process of prevention. We will never be able to justify or disseminate successful programs if we lack sound evaluative data. Both the people involved in the change effort and those who provide the resource base are owed information as to whether the program "worked." While evaluation can consist of methodologically sophisticated elements, what this discussion provides is a non-technical, yet sound, statement of the features of evaluation that can be incorporated into an overall community change process. Such an evaluation takes the politically sound position that the starting point is with the local program effort. Thus, while another evaluation might, and perhaps should, be conducted by an outside group, an assumption is made here that within the whole process of community development a primary emphasis must be given to evaluation and assessment. Once again the principle of ownership arises, in this case with an insistence that primary responsibility for evaluation be vested within the local group that is carrying out the program. Evaluation is too important to leave totally to outside "experts."

Seven, the book is readable. The text is a result of many years of experience with formats and presentations, out of which elements emerge which become readily understood and interpreted. The basic ideas have gone through many siftings and revisions. The logical core of the book reflects ideas that have been progressively hammered into shape based on what does or does not work.

In sum, this is assuredly a book for the 1980s. Here is an alternative to the politics of despair and cynicism which pervades so much of current thinking about youth problems and their prevention. Whatever the complex and tangled processes that lead to youthful alienation and rebellion, ultimately it comes down to local young people acting out their misbehavior in local contexts. This book argues that these local contexts provide a starting point for prevention utilizing strategies of youth and community development. Above all else, its optimistic premise is that the task can be done, based on the assumption that we can, and should, hold out hope to the young people of our communities.

Melbourne, Australia
July, 1983

preface

This book has been a long time in the making. It is the result of more than 30 years of personal experience, extensive interaction with many people and, more recently, frequent experiences in leading workshops focused upon prevention strategies in a number of states and local communities.

The personal experience goes back to my own family life while growing up, to college days and to some memorable events which took place during summers of volunteer work with the American Friends Service Committee in this country and in Europe. It also includes some involvement in community change before and during the civil rights movement in the south.

After entering the field of social work and seeing the overwhelming emphasis on remedial activity within that profession, I began early in my professional life to question our always being so reactive. After-the-fact help to people who hurt is good, but would it not be better to confront the sources of the hurt? I found this to be a question worth pondering, exploring and building a career around.

For the past 14 years I have been more specifically involved in prevention programs, and for 10 years have been responsible for providing technical assistance to organizations, communities and states focused on developing effective prevention strategies.

Though my work in prevention began with a specific focus on the symptom of juvenile delinquency, it became apparent very soon that to confine one's concern to a particular symptom creates conceptual and common-sense difficulties. We have organized human services around symptoms, building entire systems that work in relative isolation from one another. Juvenile and criminal justice, education, health, mental health, public welfare, recreation and many other services function in separate spheres and there is often isolation of components even within these systems. I came to realize that while people do in fact deplore this counterproductive condition and speak out against it, the fragmentation is really functional because those systems have been designed to react to symptoms. The fragmentation is perpetuated by the behavior of the people who control the various systems and their components. Each system comprises an industry, if you will, which seeks to maintain and expand itself. Cooperation and collaboration, while given lip-service, might break down the walls and threaten the existence of the remedial industry.

Prevention is another matter. When I have told people I have been working on a book about prevention, the immediate question has often been, "Prevention of what?" That is a logical question in a symptom-focused, remedial, reactive world. I have purposefully left any mention of symptoms out of the title of the book. One reason for this is the awareness that a wide variety of symptoms are the result of some common conditions. Designing separate systems for remedial work may make some sense, but addressing the common conditions which promote those symptoms calls for a different approach. If we can get beyond the notion that prevention is only "stopping something from happening" to a more positive approach that creates conditions which promote the well-being of people, we can begin to view human services quite differently. This, in turn, can transform and enrich our approaches to helping people and building communities that are relatively free of the symptoms we have designed our services around.

This may sound utopian and idealistic, but it is not. It is a practical matter of people becoming responsible at many levels. A generic approach to prevention which does not get caught up in remedial thought processes as has happened so much in the past frees us to use our resources more creatively and effectively.

At the risk of being presumptuous, this book is an effort to inject positive meaning into the word prevention. Many people today are assertively pursuing new and exciting approaches to building better communities. There has been strong emphasis on this in parts of the corporate world. The human potential movement spans many disciplines, professions and sectors of public and private life. I have found that my own efforts to discover the meaning of prevention have brought me into contact with many people who are on a similar quest but who may describe it in different terms. My engineer neighbor with whom I play tennis introduced me to the concept of "value engineering" which he uses in the aerospace industry, and I have joined the Society of American Value Engineers, finding there a new source of learning about positive change. John Naisbitt, in his best-selling book *Megatrends: Ten New Directions Transforming Our Lives,* gives many examples of positive change efforts. There is a widespread search for approaches to accomplishing positive ends that promote the well-being of people. For me, I expect this engaging search and the application of its discoveries to continue for a lifetime.

It is encouraging to know that a positive approach to prevention is a practical way to realize immediate, tangible results in those places where we spend our time – in our families, in classrooms, in peer groups, in neighborhoods, in the workplace, in churches, in organizations of all kinds, in decision-making groups. The technology for positive change is available to us, and we can use it if we will.

This is a book about positive change. I hope the reader who has not already done so will join the growing number of people who are thinking along the lines this book encourages. It is a most exciting world to enter.

William A. Lofquist
Tucson, Arizona
July, 1983

acknowledgments

The experience out of which this book has developed has involved many people who have made specific contributions to it. While there are far too many to name them all, there are some individuals who deserve special mention.

I am especially indebted to my colleague in Associates for Youth Development, Inc., Robert D. Cain, Jr. His skilled management, vigorous advocacy for young people, high standards and persistent encouragement have been a constant inspiration and source of direction.

My other colleagues in AYD have served as co-trainers, critics of several drafts of the manuscript, shapers of ideas, typists and strong supporters of the project. These include Theora Barringer, Lisa Brunette, Mary Cole, Teri Lopez, Dennis Maloney, John Morgenthau, Dee O'Neill and Peter Venezia. Who could ask for a better group of people with whom to work?

Others who have worked as co-trainers along the way have been Harvey Grady and Jerry Klarsfeld, two very skilled people.

Working from the east to the west coast, the following people have in one way or another assisted in the shaping of this book, and their contributions have been greatly appreciated:

David Driskill in Massachusetts; Rich Linehan in Maine; David Bundy in New Hampshire; Bill and Marilyn Albin, Robert Francis, Ruth Freymann and Joe Freeman in Connecticut; Anona Joseph, Newell Eaton, Alan Krieger and Marilyn Massick in New York; Robert Allen in New Jersey; Lawrence DeMooy in Pennsylvania; Despina Sapounakis, John Shannon, Donald Klein and Toni Francis in Maryland; Paul Keve and Tom Northen in Virginia; Ed Carr, Ken Foster, Vicky Church, Philip Cooke, Douglas Sessoms, Eleanor Lofquist, Lucille Hutaff, John Freas and Rich Maxson in North Carolina; Conrad Powell and Walter Waddell in South Carolina; James O. Chatham (with whom the first Community Development Workshop was organized) in Kentucky; Glenn Wieringa in Ohio; Glenn Stevens in Indiana; Elizabeth Arnovits in Michigan; Robert Duncan, Baron Kaylo, Frank Riley and David Dollar in Louisiana; Karen Popowski, Stan Dembouski, Mary Feerick, Sandra Hinely, Dale Free, Larry Diddier, Joseph Coughlin and Robert Dye in Illinois; Martin G. Miller in Iowa; Michael Becker, Michael Sullivan, Kathy Thorpe, Donald Percy, Philip Condu and Sylvia Patzlaff in Wisconsin; Thomas Bird and Grant Johnson in Colorado; Dee Tackett in New Mexico; Rachel MacDougall, Hila Jo Hawk, Theron Weldy, Paul Allen, Don Ijams, Frances Yerger, Ed Duperret and Ed Parmee in Arizona; George Dignan in Idaho; Kenneth Polk and Jan Elliott-Wotten in Oregon; Joseph Phelan and Sherrin Bennett in California; and Keith Wentworth in Washington.

Special thanks go to Anne W. Dosher and Sidney B. Simon, two master facilitators, for their encouragement and for being such outstanding role models.

It is a pleasure to work with such skilled and creative people as JoAnn Alwin, Barbara Sears and Ann Wilson in the production of a book. Their help has been invaluable.

A major portion of the first draft of this book was prepared under a grant from the National Institute of Juvenile Justice and Delinquency Prevention, U.S. Department of Justice. The training that was part of that program enabled us to make refinements in the training methods through six regional workshops.

It would be appropriate, though impossible, to name all of the young people and adults who have participated in the many local, statewide and regional workshops over the past 10 years. They have tested the ideas and methods that have emerged through the experience, and without them it could not have developed.

Inevitably, a book like this is influenced by many authors, trainers and others who are active in the helping professions. For me, some of the key resources of this sort are listed in the annotated bibliography at the end of the book.

Most important of all has been the constant support, encouragement and patience shown by my family through all the travel, late night and early morning writing sessions and other intrusions into our family life. My wife Mary knows the importance of this quest to me, and that makes it possible. She believes in it as much as I do.

As usual, any shortcomings in this book are the responsibility of the author.

chapter 1

What Does "Prevention" Mean?

- Crime and Delinquency
- Alcoholism
- Drug Abuse
- Mental Health Problems
- Child Abuse
- Family Problems

- Learning Problems, School Failure and Dropout
- Vandalism, Violence and Other Problem Behavior
- Teenage Pregnancy
- Stress and Burnout

Many people in a variety of fields are attempting to discover how to prevent such problems as these. Such efforts have been fragmented, because they have been focused separately upon problems that are the specific concerns of specialized interest groups. A common approach has been to react to the symptomatic behavior of individuals rather than to consider the factors which contribute to the problem behavior. Confusion about concepts, strategies and ways to evaluate results has been a serious consequence of this approach.

Making prevention practical and specific is the theme of this book. The approach is developmental; it does not prescribe "answers" or "programs" so much as it seeks to equip people with practical concepts, strategies, tools and skills through which they can determine their own paths, achieve their own results and gauge their own progress.

The immensity of the challenge of promoting a practical approach to prevention can and often does immobilize those interested in such an undertaking. Where does one begin? Who are the key people who need to be involved? How does one go about involving them? How does one generate resources for prevention in the community? What strategies might be effective? How does one know if they are working? These and many other questions tend to discourage even those who strongly believe that prevention can become a viable alternative to the usual reactive ways of doing things.

DEFINITIONS OF KEY WORDS

If a workable approach to prevention is to be developed, it will be based upon clear definitions of some key words. Several words of special importance in discussing this approach have very specific meanings, and by keeping these definitions in mind throughout our effort to discover the meaning of prevention we can work our way through some complex and often confusing conceptual and strategy concerns.

Key Words

Prevention is an active, assertive process of creating conditions and/or personal attributes that promote the well-being of people.

Remediation is a reactive, corrective effort to rectify or bring about change related to a recognized problem or need.

Community, or a "sense of community," exists when two or more people work together toward the accomplishment of mutually desirable goals (conditions).

Participation is a process of contributing to something that is meaningful and useful and being included in it. This is a key aspect of a democratic approach to change.

Alienation is a condition of separation or exclusion of a person or group of people from something that is important to them.

Collaboration is a process of participation through which people, groups and organizations work together to achieve a desirable result.

Coordination of effort is a result of collaboration.

Deterrence is an attempt to inhibit or prohibit certain activities or behaviors from occurring.

The author's intent in this book is to encourage those interested in discovering the meaning of prevention to adopt a positive, assertive attitude about what they do. A first step in this direction is to distinguish as clearly as possible between prevention and remediation as they have been defined. Some clear and important differences exist between these two kinds of change processes, and comparing and contrasting them can help to clarify strategies.

A major portion of recent experience related to developing prevention strategies has been to repeat a common pattern: a proposal is written for a new "prevention" program, funding is obtained, and then there is yet another application of the same remedial methods that had been used before. As a result, little experimental work in prevention has occurred although a significant amount of funding has supposedly gone in that direction. We have actually learned little from these efforts. Funding agencies have contributed to this discouraging national picture because of the imprecise nature of their definitions of prevention.

As an example, in the language of "delinquency prevention" it has been fashionable to say that a new project will achieve "early identification" of the "pre-delinquent" and use methods of "early intervention" to "prevent" delinquent behavior. Many projects based upon this kind of thinking have been implemented, and the resulting activity can more appropriately be called remediation. Such an approach may, in fact, have negative results. Labeling and stigmatizing can easily occur very early in the lives of individuals who, in spite of the good intentions of service providers, may be hurt because of that labeling.

For many people the word prevention has a negative ring. It immediately suggests stopping something from happening. Indeed, that idea is included in the definition provided by *Webster's New Collegiate Dictionary*. Another emphasis is much more positive. The 1972 edition of that dictionary indicates that the derivation of the word means "to anticipate." Definitions of *prevent* include: "1a: to be in readiness for (as an occasion), b: to meet or satisfy in advance, c: to act ahead of, d: to arrive before," as well as "2: to deprive of power or hope of acting or succeeding, 3: to keep from happening or existing, 4: to hold or keep back"[1]

The working definition for prevention being proposed emphasizes the idea of actively creating conditions which would preclude the occurrence of the symptoms one wishes to avoid. Thus the emphasis is on promoting the well-being of people through positive action that changes the conditions under which the behaviors to be prevented are most likely to occur.

The idea of stopping something from happening is more directly approached through another strategy, suggested by the word *deterrence.* Deterrence, as will be demonstrated, is a remedial strategy. Distinguishing between prevention and remedies is important to conceptualizing, planning and designing strategies for a wide variety of human service activities.

ARENAS OF HUMAN SERVICE ACTIVITY: PUTTING PREVENTION IN CONTEXT

If people are to discover and use practical, workable and effective approaches to prevention, they must first be able to identify and distinguish between various types of human service activity. "Human service" is viewed in a very broad sense. It includes many efforts, public and private, professional and voluntary, formal and informal, that seek to meet the needs of people. These efforts include the service activities that occur in and through educational, justice, recreational, health and mental health, religious, economic, and other governmental and civic institutions and organizations.

The framework presented here takes two features of a human service activity into consideration. These are the *purpose* and the *focus* of the activity.

The Purpose Continuum

The purpose of a particular human service activity can be stated in many ways. The Purpose Continuum presented here uses as its opposite ends the words *prevention* and *remediation* as they have been defined.

Every human service activity has a purpose, and for planning and action it is important to state clearly what that purpose is. On the Purpose Continuum of this framework can be seen human service activities that extend from the most positive and assertive efforts to create conditions and personal attributes that promote the well-being of people, at one end, to the reactive, corrective efforts of remediation, at the other. Seeing these activities in relation to a continuum provides for the possibility that a particular service design will include some preventive and some remedial features, thus falling somewhere near the middle of the continuum.

The Focus Continuum

The focus of human service activity can also be described in many ways. In their helpful book, *Consultation,*[2] Blake and Mouton describe several *units of change.* These include the individual, group, intergroup, organization and the larger social system. This listing is useful, and each of these units of change can appropriately be placed on the Focus Continuum in logical order. We might also add such words as family, peer group, neighborhood and other descriptions that denote tangible and definable entities that serve as foci of human service activity.

In this framework the two words that are used to describe the ends of the Focus Continuum are *individual* and *conditions.*

Obviously, much human service activity is focused upon the individual. As we move beyond the individual to consider the various relationships that people become engaged in and the circumstances under which these relationships occur, the word "conditions" becomes useful. This refers to a set of circumstances that in some way is important. These might be conditions within a family, a school classroom, a neighborhood, a labor union, a city council, a human service agency or any grouping of people or situation around which clear boundaries can be established for action purposes. The relevant characteristics of those conditions for change purposes can usually be described by the people involved. A focus on conditions makes it possible to deal with some strategic aspects of human service activity that the more traditional approaches to human services have tended to deemphasize, discourage or avoid.

The Focus Continuum becomes useful as ways are considered to shape service activities in order to obtain desirable results. The changes sought through human service activity involve changes in behavior on someone's part. The usual focus on "client" change is useful up to a point, but the limited concept of the "helper-client" relationship is descriptive of only a portion, and a relatively small one, of human service activity.

Other common ways of describing relationships in human service organizations are "provider-recipient," "teacher-student," "doctor-patient," "probation officer-probationer," and "leader-participant." All of these pairs of words describe transactions in which there is a giver and a recipient, a person with solutions and a person with problems or needs. These kinds of "subject-object" relationships have more relevance in some types of human service activity than in others. It can be generalized that, as human service activity is currently designed, activities which are remedial in nature require this type of transaction. The relationships most appropriate for preventive service activity may well call for a different quality of relationship among resource people, a difference to be explored in detail.

The Four Quadrants of Human Service Activity

By using the Purpose and Focus Continua it becomes possible to identify four specific arenas of human service activity, as illustrated in Figure 1. The Purpose Continuum is placed across the top of the square, and the Focus Continuum along the left margin. Four arenas of human service activity result from this juxtaposition:

QUADRANT 1 – This is preventive activity which focuses on conditions, and is called "Community Development."

QUADRANT 2 – This is preventive activity which focuses on individuals, and is called "Personal Growth and Development."

QUADRANT 3 – This is remedial activity which focuses on conditions, and is called "Community Problem Solving."

QUADRANT 4 – This is remedial activity which focuses on individuals, and is called "Personal Problem Solving."

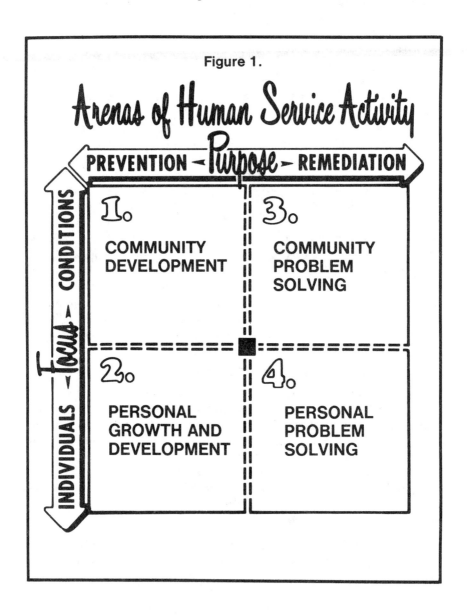

Figure 1.

Arenas of Human Service Activity

PREVENTION ← *Purpose* → REMEDIATION

CONDITIONS

Focus

INDIVIDUALS

1. COMMUNITY DEVELOPMENT

3. COMMUNITY PROBLEM SOLVING

2. PERSONAL GROWTH AND DEVELOPMENT

4. PERSONAL PROBLEM SOLVING

The four arenas represent four equally important parts of a balanced human service system, quite unlike the present reality in human services at all levels (local, state and national) where the emphasis is predominantly remedial and concentrated in the individual arena (Quadrant 4). Assessing this reality is an important step in developing strategies for creating more effective human service resources. At the present time much human service activity is based on the continuation of traditional patterns of service-providing behavior rather than on the design of strategies to attain legitimate service goals. There are many reasons for this unfortunate circumstance. The use of this framework can help in an examination of the situation, and thus help to clarify the task of discovering the meaning of prevention.

A brief description of the characteristics of each quadrant helps to categorize the wide range of human service activity.

Community Development (Quadrant 1) Activities having prevention as their purpose and focusing on conditions are in the Community Development Arena. Positive efforts which seek to enhance the well-being of people through purposefully and assertively bringing about changes in specific conditions are included here. This will probably involve organizational and institutional change. The primary emphasis of this book is to shift more attention and resources to this arena because of a belief that this quadrant deserves a much higher priority among the four arenas than it receives at present. Not only are its benefits relatively unexplored within human services, but activity in this arena can have significant positive impact in the other three arenas. This is currently the least understood, least emphasized and least clearly defined of the four arenas.

Some of the specific service strategies characteristic of Quadrant 1 are community assessment, community planning, community education, community organization, organization development consultation, training, advocacy (for changes in conditions), and legislation and policy development.

Personal Growth and Development (Quadrant 2) Positive, assertive efforts to promote personal growth and development with individuals are placed here. Group experiences are commonly structured as the primary strategy for these activities. They might focus on the development of leadership and decision-making skills, technical skills of various kinds, relationship skills, positive self concepts and other benefits which, it is believed, enhance the individual. A number of traditional organizations, frequently referred to as "character building" programs, have concerned themselves with the activities of this quadrant, using recreation and education focused groups as a strategy.

Schools have also focused attention here. In a real sense any educational experience is a personal growth experience insofar as it promotes personal well-being. The controversy about the relative importance of the "cognitive" and "affective" domains in educational theory and practice has long been an educational problem area, and educational policy is often established in relation to community pressure around these issues. Equipping people with usual academic skills and subjects creates no problem, but such areas as family life education, values clarification, relationship and decision-making skills seem to generate conflicts in the community that affect the ways policy is shaped. The language of this controversy, using such terms as "back to the basics," is frequently unclear about what, indeed, is basic.

Another way of viewing personal growth and development is to consider the kinds of experiences which promote positive self concepts and enhance a sense of self worth. For example, the ability to get and hold a job is important in our society. So job readiness training may be seen as providing an important personal growth experience, as does the actual job experience itself.

The Personal Growth and Development Arena is an arena in which many "natural" experiences occur in everyday life. It is also an important arena for human service activity. Because it lies on the preventive part of the Purpose Continuum it deserves special attention if human service resources are to be used positively in a manner that reduces the need for after-the-fact remedial activity and promotes positive personal development.

Community Problem Solving (Quadrant 3) Conditions that have created problems and require some kind of corrective or remedial action lie in the Community Problem Solving Arena. These conditions may be organizational or institutional in scope; they may occur in a neighborhood or more generally in a specific geographical area. The response to them is essentially reactive because there is a recognized need that requires corrective action.

Conditions that may stimulate activity in this arena are high unemployment, a rise in the crime rate, a high incidence of child abuse, widespread drug and alcohol abuse, a lowering of academic achievement scores, epidemic health problems, violence and vandalism in a neighborhood and many others. The word "deterrence" as defined above will describe some activities of this quadrant. When some kind of problem that affects many people is seen as reaching crisis proportions, the activities of this arena may be called into play. This may be characterized as "the squeaky wheel gets the grease" approach. Frequently the intensity of corrective activity will subside as the sense of crisis subsides, leaving the root causes of the crisis untouched, only to give rise to the appearance of urgency at a later time.

The need for community problem solving action is sometimes a subject of controversy, depending upon conditions in the community. For example, conditions of race and sex discrimination may exist for a long time, but unless someone calls attention to them they do not become the focus of community problem solving activity. When action is initiated to change the condition, the strategies used are often controversial and generate resistance to change.

Personal Problem Solving (Quadrant 4) This arena includes individual treatment and various kinds of remedial efforts related to particular needs or problems. Activities of this arena usually are focused on individual change, but individuals are often involved as members of a group in order to promote change. Such strategies as group therapy, family treatment, group homes and remedial work with individuals in a group classroom setting are examples of using the dynamics of the group to assist individuals. These strategies are also used to address some important aspects of relationship problems as individuals experience them.

Educational programs which prepare people for the various helping professions focus more attention on this arena than on the other three. The skills of individual counseling are the predominant focus of these programs. Many human service organizations are designed as Quadrant 4 service agencies. Their stated purposes, the job descriptions of staff members and their service patterns are clearly directed toward individual remediation. The predominance of this arena in both professional education programs and in patterns of service organization design is a reality that greatly affects an effort to discover the meaning of prevention.

Illustrating the Four Quadrants

The activities of the four quadrants are certainly not mutually exclusive. There is much overlapping, and certain skills and strategies can be used in each of the arenas. One such basic skill is the ability to listen and hear with discernment. The lines in the figure which indicate the four quadrants are dotted rather than solid to suggest the interplay that occurs between and among them. At the same time there are important contrasts.

The language of human services often makes use of the words "direct services," and their user usually is thinking of Quadrant 4 activity. Such use betrays both a lack of understanding of the other three quadrants and tends to leave others who might not know better with the impression that the service activities of the other three arenas are somehow "indirect." It is important to see the wide range of service options available through all four quadrants as *direct services*. This means that well designed services in all arenas can have direct, measurable impact in relation to their objectives. It means that they all involve direct work with people in the pursuit of short and long range results.

A Case Example: "The Principal's Referral"

To illustrate the four quadrants, a common experience called "The Principal's Referral" is useful. The phone rings in the offices of Sunshine Youth Agency, and it is Mr. Smith, principal of Southside Junior High School who calls: Ms. Jones, eighth grade teacher, has brought Johnny to the office. Johnny hit another student in the classroom. He has also been missing school regularly, has done little work, is suspected of using drugs and alcohol and, according to Ms. Jones, is "hanging around with the wrong crowd." Mr. Smith sees Johnny as headed for further trouble and decides to refer Johnny to Sunshine Youth Agency. How should the person who answers the phone respond to Mr. Smith's request for help? Is a Quadrant 1, a Quadrant 2, a Quadrant 3, or a Quadrant 4 response most appropriate or is it possible to shape an even better response that includes some elements of two or more quadrants?

One might say that this situation, by its very nature, requires a remedial response, automatically pointing toward Quadrants 3 and 4. One might say further that, since Johnny is an individual and obviously has a problem, a Quadrant 4 response with Johnny as the client is the only reasonable option. It can be argued, however, that there are attractive choices to be made in each of the quadrants, and that a Quadrant 4 response may be the least attractive. Not a small consideration is the possibility that Mr. Smith may have clear expectations that Sunshine will make a Quadrant 4 response. If, in addition, Sunshine advertises itself as a "counseling agency," and all of its professional staff members have been trained as counselors, the response to Mr. Smith is probably predetermined as a Quadrant 4 response, leading to a referral and giving little consideration to other alternatives.

A Quadrant 4 response, though, could have some potentially negative outcomes. First, it removes Johnny from the mainstream of his school and, depending upon how the situation is handled, may be another experience in negative labeling for him. He is, in fact, being rejected by the school as "too difficult to handle." Second, accepting Johnny as a Quadrant 4 referral may relieve the school of its responsibility for Johnny by making it unnecessary for school personnel to make an effort to deal with Johnny in a constructive manner *in the school.*

An automatic Quadrant 4 response also would rule out or discourage consideration of some of the other, potentially creative responses within the other quadrants. It may be, for example, that there are a number of other students like Johnny in the school, that a number of factors are contributing to disruptive student behavior and that a Quadrant 3 response that emphasizes community problem solving with a focus on those factors would be the service of choice. Another possibility may be that Ms. Jones is one of several teachers who make numerous referrals to the principal's office and who seem unable to work effectively with disruptive students. In that case a Quadrant 3 response that would provide special training for those teachers in better classroom management techniques would be helpful. This would support her in using better ways of relating to Johnny without removing him from the classroom, and without *singling her out as a less-than-adequate teacher.*

Still another consideration could be introduction of new curriculum methods that help students learn new relationship skills, handle their frustrations more constructively and experience positive approaches to problem solving. This kind of Quadrant 2 approach could benefit many other students in addition to Johnny, contribute to the overall improvement of student discipline, enrich the teachers' teaching experience, and better equip the students for community living.

If the response to the referral were to involve a conference with Mr. Smith, it is possible that while talking about Johnny a skillful consultant might listen to Mr. Smith's concerns about the school and its approach to disruptive student behavior. A sensitive listener might learn about some of the internal dynamics of the school as an organization and present to Mr. Smith some ways that the school climate might be improved, teacher morale boosted, faculty teamwork enhanced, student involvement in shaping the school environment promoted and Mr. Smith's satisfaction with his job heightened. Such a Quadrant 1 approach may sound like fantasy, but it is not an unrealistic possibility if the service provider has the proper skills. The call about Johnny might well be the occasion for attending to some clearly related and broader considerations that have the potential for *creating conditions that promote the well-being of all the people related to the school.* (See the Note below.)

Note

The literature of prevention in the human services field has been dominated by concepts borrowed from the public health field that use the terms "primary" prevention, "secondary" prevention and "tertiary" prevention. Since these terms are so recurrent in discussion about prevention, they should be mentioned, if only for the purpose of suggesting that they have confused and distracted efforts to discover the meaning of prevention. Indeed, any activity can be described as prevention through the use of these terms. Everything from "lollypops to lobotomies" have been claimed to be prevention strategies.

While these terms denoting three types of action have been used in legitimate attempts to clarify the meaning of prevention, much of the discussion has been either obscure and highly academic or has been used to justify the use of remedial methods as prevention. A cynical observation would point to the fact that this language has also been used to attract funds allocated for "prevention" while remedial strategies have been used in their expenditure.

Experience has shown that much discussion about prevention has used the term "primary prevention" to refer to "real prevention" while "secondary" and "tertiary" prevention have in reality been remediation as defined above. These terms, therefore, will not be used in this book.

Those who are so inclined might wish to make a distinction between "primary, secondary and tertiary remediation" in relation to the service activities of Quadrant 4 (Personal Problem Solving) to describe activities that are increasingly reactive.

This brief exploration of the use of the four quadrant figure in relation to one simple situation suggests that current ways of designing human service activities may well lack imagination, have less relevance to common situations than they might and, unwittingly or by default, pursue some of the less attractive service options. It also suggests that a well designed service approach to a particular situation might at best include several kinds of activities that fall within two, three or even all four quadrants. It suggests, further, that careful analysis of the various aspects of the situation can lead to creative approaches in the two preventive quadrants that might have far-reaching results that go much beyond those of current service patterns. Discovering the meaning of prevention has the potential of leading community groups into such a creative realm. There are many forces which stand in the way, however, and we will examine some of them as we proceed.

Some other comparisons and contrasts help to illustrate the use of the framework and to set the stage for further exploration of the rich potential of prevention. Obviously, good listening, communication and analytical skills are needed for effective work in all four quadrants. Working in each of the arenas requires the ability to relate effectively person-to-person. Work with groups can also take place in all of the arenas, calling for insight into group dynamics and skill in using them.

Generalizations used for comparing and contrasting the arenas need to be made with care, but they can be useful for illustrative purposes. Quadrant 4 service activity is usually guarded with confidentiality and is a private transaction, while work in the other three quadrants entails public transactions that invite participation and public awareness. In a real sense, this means that activity in Quadrants 1, 2 and 3 may require more risk-taking because it is more public. Much Quadrant 4 activity happens behind closed doors, and *the burden for change rests with the client.* In Quadrants 1 and 3 the burden for change rests with a number of people and is particularly dependent upon those who can exercise some control over the conditions that need to be changed. This may well help to explain why Quadrant 4 enjoys so much attention while there often is reluctance to venture into Quadrants 1 and 3. After all, Quadrant 4 service options do not challenge the *status quo* of the community, the organization providing the remedial service or the referral agent.

Another important possibility is that an initial service response may begin in one of the remedial quadrants and, with careful positive planning, those responsible may shift the focus into one or both of the preventive quadrants. People who work in organizations designed for Quadrant 4 activity have frequently indicated that their pursuit of service goals has taken them into the other quadrants. Often they state they had not conceptualized what they were doing very clearly and that the framework provides a rationale for what they have done. One purpose of the framework is to assist people in considering the options available to them more objectively and at earlier points in the planning of the strategy.

The purpose of this book is to develop a rationale for community development (Quadrant 1) as a condition-focused prevention strategy. Approaching prevention from a Quadrant 4 mindset has in the past severely limited efforts to discover the meaning of prevention. This book is intended to demonstrate that approaching service activity in all four quadrants from a Quadrant 1 mindset has much to offer for the challenging task of designing human services, especially in a shrinking economy. Quadrant 1's condition-focused prevention emphasis has some positive qualities that the other three quadrants do not possess, which suggests *that* quadrant may be a beginning point and a basis for planning human services.

COMMON ATTITUDES ABOUT PREVENTION

Many people are skeptical about the practicality of effecting change through prevention. These attitudes are honest and are often held by persons genuinely interested in prevention. Sincere skepticism must be recognized, for to acknowledge, face and overcome it is to discover a positive and practical approach to prevention. The "Common Attitudes about Prevention" listed below are balanced by a set of contrasting statements which describe "Characteristics of Effective Prevention Strategies."

COMMON ATTITUDES ABOUT PREVENTION	CHARACTERISTICS OF EFFECTIVE PREVENTION STRATEGIES
1. Prevention is idealistic.	1. Prevention is realistic and goal oriented.
2. Prevention is impractical and intangible.	2. Prevention is practical and specific.
3. Prevention is unmeasurable.	3. Prevention is designed to attain measurable results.
4. Prevention is only long range in nature.	4. Prevention is focused upon short and long range impact.
5. Prevention costs too much.	5. Prevention is cost effective and cost reducing.
6. Prevention is worthwhile, but we need to take care of more immediate things first.	6. Prevention is not just a luxury, but a necessity if a balanced community approach to human development is to be achieved.

Dispelling the attitudes in the first column is an important step toward discovering practical prevention strategies.

People who work in all four quadrants of human service activity can make significant contributions to an effort to discover the meaning of prevention. Indeed, it is in everyone's best interest, including those who work in the remedial quadrants, to get the see-saw in the cartoon into a proper balance. A serious effort at prevention will tamper with the economics and politics of the human service system of the community, however. It is important to examine this reality honestly and in detail if prevention is to become operational in practical and effective ways. As the cartoon suggests, if some balance in the human service resources of the community is to be achieved, some shifting in weight is needed. Does the person on the right need to lose weight in order for the one on the left to gain? Can the one on the left gain enough without taking from the remedial resources? Who is to decide? Can a *sense of community* be developed within the human service system of the community to the point that prevention can gain a balanced position? If such a change is desirable, *do human service policy groups, human service professionals and the community which supports them have the capacity to tolerate, allow and facilitate such change?*

ACTIVELY FOSTERING PREVENTION CAPACITY

It is apparent that in most communities, and certainly at the state and national levels, implementing effective prevention strategies will require a bold effort to "swim against the tide" of existing conditions and realities. The intent of this initial chapter has been to set the stage for the remainder of the book. A positive approach based upon a clear conceptualization of prevention is needed, along with sound strategies, workable tools and sharp skills, if progress is to be made toward discovering the meaning of prevention.

A useful distinction for considering this challenging task can be made between *reacting* and *activating*. To react is to respond to a need, problem or crisis after the fact. To activate, or to become *proactive,* is to take assertive action that deals with contributing or causative factors. There are qualitative, strategic, and practical differences between these two approaches that will be explored in depth in later chapters.

Considerable amounts of societal energy and resources go into reactive activity, while little emphasis is given to activating desired behavior. The reasons for this are many. The old adage that "the squeaky wheel gets the grease" is all too descriptive of the manner in which important decisions that affect people daily in many ways are made. It is also descriptive of the manner in which human service programs are most often designed. A critical factor in the quest for discovering the meaning of prevention is the quality of leadership that exists in the community. This includes not only the leadership abilities of those in positions of responsibility in public office and in the administrative and management roles of service organizations, but the leadership skills of citizens who are concerned about their community. Developing leadership for active, assertive efforts to bring about positive change that results in the creation of new conditions which are free of the symptomatic behaviors one wishes to prevent is a focal issue in this approach to prevention.

A key question to be explored is "Can people become responsible, within realistic limits, for shaping the conditions under which they live, work, learn, use their leisure and otherwise spend their time?" This question can be given a positive answer if people have practical concepts about change, relevant tools and strategies, and can build a team of key people to support one another in developing a prevention strategy.

Discovering the meaning of prevention as a practical approach to positive community change can be an exciting and engaging experience. It can help to break negative, confining patterns that often are the earmarks of organizational and community life. If even a small number of people can achieve success in some limited ways, they can gain the confidence and skill to confront more challenging realities which seem to defy solution.

A community development approach to prevention has a way of "turning people on" to positive action. It is an antidote to apathy and uncertainty and it can boost the morale of those who have become discouraged about the possibilities of making things better. Perhaps even more important, it can bring people together in an experience of shared responsibility for community betterment.   □

chapter 2
Basic Ideas For Building Prevention Capacity

Discovering the meaning of prevention is a difficult and complex process that requires practical and productive experiences for those involved. Unless the process has tangible results that can be observed and appreciated, it is of little value.

The real test of an approach to prevention or any other important human service endeavor is whether or not it works. Does it achieve the desired results? Does it make sense? Does it point toward clear and specific steps to be taken? Does it provide a language that people can use for intelligible communication? Does it provide a framework which helps people to organize their resources, focus their energies and gauge their progress? Does it help to inspire and stimulate people to take personal risks and change the *status quo* to more desirable conditions?

The kind of change process that prevention requires is at once a personal and a social matter. It is personal in that individuals are challenged to examine and possibly change their values, attitudes and behavior. It is social because it has implications for groups of people, organizations and institutions. To stand the test of workability, the prevention effort not only requires those involved to become both personally and organizationally accountable, but it also demands accountability on the part of the community where it takes place.

Prevention is a serious matter. It is not to be taken lightly and cannot result from half-hearted gestures. An attempt to influence the values, attitudes and behavior of people, if it lacks clarity and integrity, is doomed to failure. The concepts and strategies must stand some rigid tests if they are to produce tangible results.

This book provides a framework for building prevention capacity. There is ample room for adding, enriching, modifying for local use and creating new ideas and materials within this framework. Indeed, the reader is encouraged to use the book as such a stimulus for developing an approach that creatively fits the conditions where it is applied.

A VALIDITY TEST FOR WORKABLE PREVENTION STRATEGIES

In order to build practical and effective prevention strategies, the following five criteria can serve as a test of workability. It is suggested that the reader subject any ideas about prevention, including those in this book, to these criteria.

Workable Strategies for Prevention Are:

I. *Engaging*

The approach from the beginning needs to get and hold people's attention and interest.

II. *Sound in Concept*

The approach needs to make sense, provide a clear rationale, and stand up to scrutiny over time.

III. *Easy to Communicate*

The approach should provide a language that is easy to use and that enables people to keep in touch with one another and interpret what is happening to others.

IV. *Skill Oriented*

The approach should equip people with workable skills that are easily taught and readily usable.

V. *Results Oriented*

The approach should lead to tangible action that is based upon a realistic assessment of both current and desired conditions and is capable of attaining the latter.

There has been a tendency in the literature of prevention toward a level of obscurity that implies that prevention is the province of a group of highly trained and isolated professionals. Such is not the case. Practical prevention strategies invite the participation of those to whom the matter at hand is important. Sound and clearly developed principles are not obscure but, rather, are capable of communication in everyday language. Indeed, as ideas become more refined they become easier to communicate in clear and efficient language.

SOME POSITIVE VALUES UNDERGIRDING PREVENTION ACTIVITY

The approach to prevention advocated here is based upon several fundamental beliefs. These can be viewed as basic positive values undergirding prevention activity.

One of these, suggested at the end of the preceding chapter in the form of a question, is restated declaratively here:

> *People can become responsible, within realistic limits, for shaping the conditions under which they live, work, learn, use their leisure and otherwise spend their time.*

This basic value suggests that, while everyone is restrained by realities of various kinds, the circumstances surrounding every individual permit some latitude for responsible individual action that can impact or influence the conditions of that individual's environment. It also points toward the notion that individuals, working in concert, can shape, through responsible action, the conditions that are important to them. Applied to prevention, this suggests a belief that people collectively can create conditions which are increasingly free of the symptoms or factors they wish to prevent.

> *People are their own best resources for bringing about change which is important to them.*

This basic value is intended to communicate respect for the potential of the individual to become an active and effective participant in a process of planned change. It also suggests that every individual is potentially a resource person. This has implications for the attitudes of promoters of change toward their potential allies. It also provides a basis for treating people as colleagues and resources *(subjects)* to be engaged for what they have to offer and not as targets *(objects)* to be changed.

> *Participation by people in shaping the conditions that affect them promotes ownership and vested interest in the change being sought and increases commitment to seeing that the change is achieved and maintained.*

Throughout this book the ideas of participation in change and sharing in the solution to problems will be emphasized. To illustrate, if delinquent behavior is the focus of concern, this value suggests that the delinquent person may be considered to be among the key resource people to be engaged in the prevention of delinquency. This begins to point away from the traditional "helper-client" kind of relationship toward one in which new alliances for change are developed.

> *It is desirable to promote change through the use of the existing human, physical and financial resources of the community.*

This basic value suggests that existing resources can best be used to promote the change that is desired. While new financial resources or reallocation of some funds may be needed to implement prevention activities, this value points toward an effort to use what is already at hand more effectively.

An application of this value can point toward a primary emphasis upon engaging the community's people resources and reducing the need for financial resources. Such an emphasis reflects more than a healthy concern for national economic trends; it acknowledges that it just makes good sense to solve problems more effectively at lower costs. This implies more strategic use of existing resources. The question—"How can we get better use from what we have?"—is appropriate to keep in the forefront throughout the progress of a prevention effort.

A commitment to this value can also help to avoid the distracting task of searching for new funds. A group of people who begin with an assumption that they will achieve a goal without additional money can design some most creative strategies for obtaining results.

Prevention is essentially a local activity that focuses upon local conditions and concerns that affect people locally.

Seeing prevention as a process that affects people in the local community makes it possible to clarify the roles and responsibilities of people at the local, state and national levels for fostering prevention capacity. It also places the basic responsibility squarely where it belongs—in the community where people live.

These five statements provide the value base upon which this approach to prevention rests. Elaborations upon these statements will be found throughout the book. The concepts and strategies being proposed are built upon a value-laden philosophy about people, the community and change processes. It is important to acknowledge this value base and to keep it in the forefront.

THE ESSENTIAL ELEMENTS OF A CHANGE PROCESS

Prevention is an active process of planned change which leads to a new condition that is relatively free of the symptoms one wishes to prevent. Change is also needed within the human service system if prevention is to become a part of a balanced use of human service resources. Change, then, is the focus of our attention, so it becomes useful to consider the essential elements of a change process. Many efforts to solve problems or bring about desirable change fail because the people involved fail to go through some basic steps on their way to finding solutions.

These considerations will be given fuller treatment in Chapter V, but it is important to introduce them here as part of setting the stage for getting a prevention program under way.

There are three questions which suggest the essential elements of a change process:

—Where are you now? (Condition A)
—Where do you want to be? (Condition B)
—How will you get there? (→)

The first question asks for a clarification of the current situation, or the *status quo*. This will be referred to throughout the book as "Condition A." A description of Condition A needs to be specific and detailed enough so the people involved have a clear idea of what it is they are trying to change. This is also necessary if they are to know later whether or not the change has, in fact, taken place. In other words, has the prevention program worked? (The importance of evaluation becomes clear from the very beginning!)

The second question asks for a clarification of the situation that is desired, or the *goal*. This will be referred to hereafter as "Condition B." Here again, a description of Condition B needs to be specific and detailed enough so the people involved have a clear idea of what it is they want to accomplish. This, too, is necessary if they are to know whether or not the desired change has occurred.

The third question asks for a clarification of the methods that will be used to bring about the change from Condition A to Condition B. In illustrations of the change process that will be used at several points, the methods or strategies for prevention will be represented by an (→).

Using these simple symbols, the essential elements of a change process look like this:

$$A \rightarrow B$$

Of course, planned change is not a simple matter, but it is important to be able to identify these basic parts of the process and to keep them in sequence, in order to recognize clearly when something is being left out or not receiving enough attention to solve the problem.

WARNING TO THE READER!

If there is a temptation to think of this as simplistic and too elementary, *do not be deceived!* Millions of dollars and untold amounts of human energy have been expended on activity that began nowhere because the perpetrators started with a set of activities and did not clarify where they were or where they wanted the activities to take them.

The logical sequence of combining these essential elements is (1) to figure out and describe in clear and specific terms the condition to be changed, (2) to decide what new condition should be brought about, and (3) to design a set of action steps that has the potential of getting from the one place to the other. *The third can take place only after the first two have been accomplished!* The tendency to move into activities without clarifying objectives is what Dr. George Odiorne has called "the activity trap."[3]

In the example of "The Principal's Referral" in Chapter I, it is important to determine first what the problem (Condition A) is and what the desired result (Condition B) is before designing a set of steps to get there. Because of this, it would be a mistake to jump into the activities of any of the four quadrants before undertaking these first two basic steps. If a referral resource, such as Sunshine Youth Agency, has a predetermined response to all referrals, such as counseling, regardless of the circumstances being considered, then it is probable that the agency is caught in an activity trap. Obviously, many human service organizations are caught in the activity trap, and part of our task, if we are to promote an interest in prevention, is to extricate them from that trap so their resources can be used to best advantage. The ability of an organization or group of people to move freely toward the arena of human service activity that can best accomplish the most desirable goals in a specific situation is, indeed, a worthy condition to have exist.

This faces us with a dilemma, for the ways by which many human service organizations have been designed often do not afford them that freedom. This is the result of a number of forces which shape human service organizations. If more balance is to be brought about in the way human service resources and other community resources are used, it is important that we understand those forces and learn to confront them in a way that leads to more emphasis on prevention. This is in essence a political process, for it has to do with the changing and shaping of policy at the local, state and national levels. It also involves change in organizational and institutional patterns, many of which are maintained by long-standing tradition and community inertia.

A simple example can help to illustrate the use of these three essential elements of a change strategy. The author was working with the faculty of an elementary school interested in using these elements as a basis for improving their school. The matter of student behavior on the bus to and from school each day was selected as the focus of their attention. In describing the current situation (Condition A), it was pointed out that the noise level on the bus was so high that on one occasion the bus driver was unable to hear the siren of an emergency vehicle, creating a dangerous situation. Several other observations focused specifically on the students' behavior. As the faculty members were encouraged to shape other descriptive statements, they continued to describe the unacceptable behavior of the students. Several probing questions were then asked that focused more on the conditions under which the students ride the bus. This led to other kinds of observations, such as: "There is little communication between school staff and the bus drivers." "Bus drivers have little orientation and training related to handling student behavior," "Standards for 'acceptable' behavior on the bus have not been established." "School staff members do not know how the students view the situation on the buses." "No positive incentives for 'acceptable' behavior on the buses have been established." "Students have not been involved in helping to establish and maintain 'acceptable' behavior on the buses."

As these insights were posted before the group, they began to get a sense of some goals they would like to establish. It became obvious that desirable goals could be shaped by some rewording of the Condition A statements they had developed. They quickly began to move toward this, and a strategy for dealing with the situation began to emerge.

In it interesting to note that while their first inclination had been to focus on the "unacceptable" behavior of the students, the more useful Condition A statements focused on matters that were the result of adult behavior, and their strategies that emerged from their Condition B statements were aimed at positive changes in adult behavior. Within two or three days from this meeting they began to notice a difference in student behavior, and after several weeks they were satisfied that they had achieved a significant improvement in the situation. It is also interesting to note that this new approach created a new understanding of how the school staff might approach other situations in the school.

A powerful tool for bringing about positive change is to begin with the task of describing the conditions under which unacceptable behavior is occurring. Even a complex set of circumstances can be described in clear, simple sentences. Assisting a group of people who view those circumstances from various vantage points to develop these descriptive statements is a valuable helping role and a necessary first step toward building a prevention strategy. When this understanding of Condition A has emerged, then useful goals (Condition B) can be established and the groundwork for shaping effective strategies has been achieved.

SOME BASIC ASSUMPTIONS FOR PREVENTION

Discovering the meaning of prevention and taking steps to bring prevention activities into balance with remedial activities requires a clear sense of direction among an expanding number of people at the local community level. If this is to be a group effort, it is important that those who work together operate from the same or very similar basic assumptions. The failure to clarify these assumptions can result in working at cross purposes, a waste of valuable resources, and ultimately in failure to achieve the desired objectives. Many change efforts have foundered because early clarification of assumptions was not achieved among the core action group.

The following assumptions are focused upon positive *youth* development and the prevention of the kinds of problems faced by young people. They are examples of the kinds of statements that can serve to focus a group's attention. They also embody certain beliefs about the nature of social institutions and their relationship to a population such as the young people of the community.

Basic Assumptions about Youth Development and the Prevention of Youth Problems

1. Youth problems and their prevention are community problems and responsibilities, and both the contributing factors and the solutions are to be found in the community.

2. As a community responsibility, the prevention of youth problems involves bringing about change in those conditions which contribute to youth problems.

3. A balanced community approach to youth development includes both the provision of legitimate remedial services and an emphasis upon creating conditions which contribute to the well-being of young people.

4. Changing community conditions that contribute to youth problems usually requires changes in organizations and institutions in the community. This requires a cooperative effort on the part of decision makers, human service professionals and youth and adult citizens.

5. Community, organizational and institutional change requires a combination of useful concepts, purposive strategies and effective leadership skills. At best, these are shared by an expanding group of people who work together.

6. Resources at the state and national levels can be supportive of the kind of community responsibility required for positive youth development. It is important that resources at those levels do not stand in the way and act as restraining forces, as they frequently do.

As a group of people embark upon a process of planned change they will do well from time to time to reconsider their basic assumptions. The clarity of these assumptions and the knowledge that members of the group are together in their belief in and commitment to the assumptions serve as a source of strength for the group. For this reason, the assumptions should be placed beside the basic values which undergird the work of the group, for together they serve as the underpinnings of the approach to a very difficult and challenging endeavor.

While the assumption statements just presented are focused upon young people, similar statements can also be developed in relation to other groupings, such as the aging, ethnic groups, and others. Actually, the kinds of positive steps that will fit our definition of prevention are steps that benefit people in general. Prevention strategies are generic in nature and can be focused upon a wide variety of symptoms and symptomatic behaviors.

A major portion of our challenge, then, is to direct more of the resources of human service organizations toward prevention. This requires organizational and institutional change. Beginning with those organizations within which people who are interested in prevention work can be useful in shaping prevention strategies. The same change strategies that are effective in fostering redirection of some of these organizations can be applied elsewhere in the larger community. Thus the organization becomes a learning and testing ground for strategies that are used in the community.

FOCUSING ON CONDITIONS

Using the definition of prevention as an active process of creating conditions and personal attributes that promote the well-being of people, a key consideration becomes *focusing on conditions.* "Conditions" simply refers to the circumstances that exist in a particular situation. It is possible to draw boundaries around a specific situation and describe that situation in clear and simple terms in order to deal with it. Examples are neighborhood conditions, conditions within a family, school classroom conditions, organizational conditions, or conditions in the work place. Developing insight about the importance of conditions, how they affect the people in them and how they can be changed are significant aspects of building prevention capacity.

In an effort to bring about planned change, focusing on conditions achieves several purposes. *The crucial distinction is between focusing on conditions and focusing on individuals as the primary concern of the change effort.* This distinction is part of the rationale for specifically pursuing a Quadrant 1 approach to prevention as a preferred strategy that receives primary emphasis. Even though individuals will at some point need to undergo behavioral change in order to promote change in conditions, focusing on conditions is a necessary forerunner that will encounter less resistance and lead to more positive results. The following list suggests some of the benefits that can be realized.

Benefits of Focusing on Conditions

1. Individuals are taken out of the spotlight without reducing the need for them to become responsible for their own behavior. This reduces both negative labeling of individuals and the potential for resistance to the change being sought.

2. People are encouraged to see themselves as resources for changing negative conditions to positive ones in practical and specific ways.

3. Situations are created in which every person's perspective of those conditions can become important for understanding and changing them.

4. People can become allies in working toward mutual goals. This, in turn, can reduce the potential for polarization within the group.

5. Persons who have the problem to be prevented can become resources, giving them access to positive roles, using their perspectives and encouraging them to use their energies in positive ways.

6. Joint ownership of a problem is made possible, when that is appropriate, as is joint participation in achieving a solution.

7. Boundaries useful in developing clear goals and designing specific strategies for planned change can be set.

8. Numbers of people affected by the conditions that are of concern can be directly benefited.

9. Realities involved in a problem situation can be identified with a view toward reducing "buck passing" on the part of those who can do something about the conditions.

10. Successful experiences in planned change can be carried into other condition-improving activity.

One of the greatest obstacles to discovering the meaning of prevention is the common belief that it must be, at best, a vague and nonspecific undertaking. Many people find it difficult to sort through the complex community realities that they think may be related to the "causes" of a problem. They feel overwhelmed by the variety and elusiveness of factors that may (or may not) be relevant to the symptoms they wish to prevent. *Focusing on conditions can be the key to discovering an action strategy that will bring about specific, substantive, desirable change in the community.*

Until a significant number of people, including people at policy and administrative levels of local government and in the public and private human service organizations of the community, begin to view the community from a prevention perspective, it is unlikely that regularly using prevention strategies to improve the community will gain much momentum. Preventive actions will, at best, be isolated and occasional exceptions to the usual reactive pattern unless thinking and behavior at the policy and decision levels are changed. Focusing on conditions is essential to this prevention perspective.

IDENTIFYING THE SKILLS NEEDED
FOR PREVENTION

Shaping and carrying out effective prevention strategies requires several kinds of skill and it is useful to identify some of the skills that can be used in each of the arenas of human service activity. As was stated earlier, some of these basic skills are relevant to all four quadrants of service activity. These include listening and communication skills, group leadership skills and analytical skills. The ability to translate love of, concern about and consideration for people into positive, tangible and workable strategy that gets positive results is a somewhat intangible but important kind of skill for all four quadrants.

It has proven helpful in encouraging a community development approach to prevention to consider some of the service options requiring specific skills, particularly those in Quadrants 1 and 4. Beginning with the more familiar options of Quadrant 4 is helpful for making comparisons and contrasts.

Service Options of Quadrant 4
(Personal Problem Solving)

1. Individual diagnosis.
2. Counseling, casework, psychotherapy and other individual therapeutic activities.
3. Group work and group therapy.
4. Family treatment.
5. Crisis intervention (focused on individuals).
6. Advocacy (for individuals).
7. Referral.
8. Brokerage for individual remedial services.
9. Consultation (related to individual remedial concerns).

Service Options of Quadrant 1
(Community Development)

1. Community assessment.
2. Community planning.
3. Community education.
4. Community organization.
5. Organization development consultation.
6. Training.
7. Advocacy (for changes in conditions).
8. Legislation and policy development.

These examples of specific service options serve as a partial listing of the kinds of activities that occur in these two quadrants. The overlapping nature of the quadrants is further illustrated by the recognition that many of the same service activities used in Quadrant 3 are included in the listing for Quadrant 1. This is to be expected, since both quadrants focus upon community conditions. The interplay between these two quadrants becomes clear when we consider a situation which might begin with a response to a community crisis (Quadrant 3), but then shifts toward the more positive thrust of community development (Quadrant 1) if the desire exists to improve community conditions after the crisis subsides.

The service options of community development can in large measure be carried out by trained community volunteers, some of whom may already possess some of the needed technical knowledge and skill. Human service professionals who have the technical knowledge and skills and who have a commitment to prevention will also be natural allies in developing a prevention strategy. Strong leadership is an obvious need. If prevention is to become a practical undertaking in the community it is essential that these tasks and the skills related to them are accessible to an expanding number of people, pointing to the necessity of a community prevention training program. This is described in the next section of this chapter. Community development training is one approach to equipping people with the concepts, strategies, tools and skills needed for prevention.

A more specific look at the services of Quadrant 1 helps to identify the needed skills. Chapters IV and V suggest a number of strategies and tools related to these service options.

1. *Community Assessment*

Community assessment is a process of determining and describing the current conditions (Condition A) of the community that are related to a focus of concern, such as a particular symptom. After determinining realistic boundaries around the situation to be examined, it is possible to focus specific attention upon the conditions that fall within those boundaries. Many tools and techniques are available for this kind of assessment process. Different perspectives of the conditions, provided by those who are concerned about them, can add valuable information for the assessment. For example, if the focus of attention is some aspect of a school, the perspectives of the teachers, students, administrators, support personnel, parents and others who have a vantage point will be needed. Skills for participation in the assessment process are easily taught.

2. *Community Planning*

Deciding what kinds of community conditions are desirable (Condition B) and developing ways to achieve them is an important part of achieving planned change. As groups of people develop the skills to promote positive community change they are increasing their capacity for responsible citizenship. Systematic planning processes which provide clear, step-by-step procedures allow diverse groups of people to work together in an efficient and task oriented manner.

3. *Community Education*

The level of awareness people have of existing conditions and potential approaches to planned change is a critical factor in a prevention effort.

Community education needs to be focused, specific and purposive as part of a prevention process. There are numerous ways to pursue a community education program to build community support for prevention. The various media are vehicles for general community awareness. More direct interaction with smaller groups of people can be achieved in a number of ways. At best, community education is focused upon specific prevention efforts and invites participation in those efforts.

4. *Community Organization*
As action strategies are developed as suggested in Chapter V, it becomes necessary to organize the needed community resources to achieve the desired results. A well-designed action plan will identify what needs to be done, who can best do it, what resources are needed, when the action steps will be completed and how the prevention team will know when or to what extent the goals have been achieved. Participants in the process can take part in all aspects of the organizational tasks. Careful employment of the talents and resources of the group is important.

5. *Organization Development Consultation*
Organizations of various kinds are important vehicles for providing the needed resources for carrying out prevention strategies. Organizations, however, need continually to improve their effectiveness. They may need to undergo some reorganization if they are to become involved in prevention activity. Helping organizations become more viable is a significant aspect of prevention. Organizational conditions may need to be changed in order to achieve prevention objectives. There is a growing body of knowledge about organization development that can enhance a prevention effort. The skills needed to foster and guide organizational change are rather specialized and require specific talents. While a selected few may need to carry this role, general orientation to the nature of the skills and what can be done to help organizations improve is useful to the participants in a prevention effort.

6. *Training*
Participants in a prevention process can be presumed to need specific training for the task and small group action training should be an important part of the prevention strategy. Training is both a means for increasing skill for prevention and a method for engaging people in prevention processes. Group leadership skills that can be used in small group training sessions are essential for equipping people for participation in the prevention effort, and these training sessions can become the occasion for community assessment and community planning.

7. *Advocacy (for changes in conditions)*
Advocacy for change is important in all four quadrants. It is a distinct kind of activity through which some individuals and groups of people can

become a significant part of a prevention process. Advocates will need the ability to speak clearly and persuasively with people who can exercise control over conditions and resources. While Quadrant 1 prevention activity is in a real sense a political process, the role of advocate for change also requires sensitivity, diplomacy and a good sense of timing if the results are to be positive. Being able to approach the task in a way that avoids polarization and engages people as allies is an especially valuable skill.

8. *Legislation and Policy Development*
Because policy and legal frameworks shape many of the conditions under which people live, work and learn, becoming involved in the policy and legislative process can become an important part of a prevention effort. This is especially true at the local level, but can also be useful at the state and national levels. Understanding political processes and developing the skills to influence them are critical. This includes relating to local nonprofit policy groups as well as elected governmental bodies.

The following chapters will focus specifically on how these kinds of skills can be used to have tangible impact on the kinds of symptoms about which people in a community become concerned. As people gain experience in the use of specialized skills and see that what they are doing has positive, measurable results, they begin to realize that they are developing a *technology of prevention*. This technology includes concepts, strategies, tools and skills that are aimed toward realizing specific kinds of community change. They begin to realize that not only have they acquired these skills, but they can teach them to others. In other words they can become *technical assistance providers* in their neighborhoods, schools, places of work, and through their churches, civic clubs and other organizations. As this kind of capacity builds among a growing number of people, active support groups for positive community change can become a reality. The formation of short-term technical assistance teams which are interorganizational in nature and include people with diverse vantage points who participate in different spheres of influence in the community becomes a means through which specific community conditions are addressed.

The development of specialized teams of allies is an important part of an assertive prevention strategy. Skill building is an essential part of the long range building of prevention capacity in the community.

ENGAGING KEY ALLIES FOR PREVENTION

Making prevention practical and specific requires that people work together. Depending upon the strategies that are developed, there will inevitably be times when allies are needed. The early stages of a prevention effort may be facilitated by a small nucleus of people who have a clear sense of direction. Others will be needed as the program takes shape.

The task of engaging key allies at strategic points along the way to accomplishing the various requirements of an action plan becomes crucial if the prevention effort is to succeed. Having the right people involved can obviously make the difference between success and failure.

Inviting participation is best done as part of a systematic and carefully designed approach to bringing about desired results. The following simple steps can be used at various points along the way to bring into the process persons who can help.

Engaging Key Allies

Step I List those strategic persons it is believed can be counted upon to actively support the effort.

Step II List those strategic persons it would be desirable to have involved but whose commitment to the goal may not be known.

Step III List those strategic persons who are capable of blocking the path to achieving the goal and who it is believed will not wish to participate in the effort.

These lists should be prepared carefully with clear criteria for engaging key allies in mind. It is quite possible that the people on the first list can be engaged with little persuasion, though it is crucial that a clear understanding be achieved with them about the importance and specific nature of their involvement.

The second list can include people with specialized skills, particular influence or valued perspectives. These persons might be selected to fill gaps in skill or knowledge or to supplement what is already available. An example might be someone with knowledge of and access to computer equipment to tabulate the results of a survey or to design and implement a community monitoring system.

The third list is useful for identifying where opposition might exist. On the other hand persons it is assumed will be roadblocks, when approached about the specific goals of the effort, may prove to be key allies. If people opposed to the effort can be persuaded that it is worthwhile, they, too, may become key allies. If not, they have been given a chance to participate, to react to the idea and to state clearly why they are opposed. All of this has value. Opponents may present some sound thinking to support their opposition and reveal both identities of detractors of the effort and reasons why they are opposed.

Once the lists are prepared, the people on them can be approached systematically as part of the action plan. Resource people are vitally needed, and they can be used at any point throughout the plan. It should be remembered that, while there are many forces that work against prevention, there are many resource people in every community who can be engaged.

A PRACTICAL STRATEGY – SMALL GROUP ACTION TRAINING

Several realities are usually clear whenever a person or group of people decide to undertake a program of prevention. These include: it cannot be done alone, a sense of direction is needed, people need to master certain skills, group cohesion is essential, and follow-through is necessary if success is to be achieved. Developing a strategy that attends to these realities in a practical manner is obviously a requirement.

One technique that can address all of these concerns is *small group action training.* The rationale for this technique is clear. The use of groups is an efficient way to bring selected people together to work on a task. Group meetings are an important part of our culture, though they are frequently considered unproductive or even a waste of time. The tools and strategies suggested in Chapters IV and V can provide meaningful structure to group meetings so the participants can achieve tangible results and gain a sense of satisfaction that comes from joint ownership in accomplishing an important goal. If action training is seen both as a means of equipping people with the needed tools and skills and as an occasion and opportunity to do the necessary planning for prevention, it can become an exciting and productive part of the prevention program.

For the past several years Associates for Youth Development, Inc. has been involved with a number of communities and states in using action training to promote prevention initiatives. This training has been called a "Community Development Workshop." *The purpose of the Community Development Workshop is to challenge, stimulate and engage people in planning, initiating and carrying out a systematic program of prevention in their community.* At best, it is a structured learning experience which brings together a diverse group of people who will be invited to participate in the workshop and become committed both to that effort and to active participation in various follow-up activities that are planned during the workshop.

Critical questions for the participants in a Community Development Workshop include:

- What are some key factors which cause or contribute to the problem that is of concern?

- How can problem solving and positive community change be promoted? Where are the roadblocks? Who are the potential allies?

- What are some effective strategies for changing community conditions?

- What kinds of attitudes and behaviors tend to inhibit or promote positive change, and how can they be overcome or utilized?

- How can communities save money while effectively preventing problems that are of concern?

- What leadership skills are needed for facilitating positive community change, who possesses them and how can they be further developed?

- How can a developmental process for planned change in the community be initiated and maintained?

A well designed and conducted Community Development Workshop will provide an opportunity for these kinds of questions to be explored and for a group of people to move efficiently toward the shaping and enactment of a positive prevention strategy in their community. An important consideration in designing such a workshop is that a structure and a process are provided the participants, but they have the responsibility for assessing their own community conditions, developing their own content and shaping their own directions for action.

THREE STAGES OF A WELL DESIGNED PREVENTION INITIATIVE

Since the purpose of a prevention initiative is to get tangible results, a sound plan and approach for the effort are needed. If the people involved understand from the beginning that prevention requires persistent follow-through and a support group is developed to see that the results are achieved, then the effort is more likely to succeed. A way of promoting this kind of follow-through is to recognize three stages of a well designed prevention initiative. Participants can gauge their progress in a general way by using the characteristics of these stages:

Stage I – Orientation, Training and Planning

This is a preparation stage. It is a time during which the initial action group is formed and becomes familiar with the concepts, strategies, tools and skills of prevention. Action plans are shaped in this stage and a growing commitment to the undertaking is in evidence. Key people are engaged and buy into the goals of the effort. The core group begins to show evidence of the ability to sell others on the concepts and enlist their support in pursuing the goals that have been established. This stage ends when a strong move toward implementation of the action plan becomes evident.

Stage II – Implementation and System Impact

This stage is an action stage. It consists primarily of putting the action plan into place, gaining support for seeing that the plan works, building the capacity to gauge the progress of the action steps and doing the necessary trouble-shooting to see that the plan is working properly. As a prevention strategy is implemented, especially with Quadrant 1 efforts, there will probably be some impact upon various systems in the community as those systems are engaged in the action steps. For example, if the focus is on delinquency prevention, organizations that exist to deal with that symptom will necessarily be involved. A shift toward prevention will probably have some impact on the justice system of which such organizations are a part. Planned involvement will require some changes in those systems, so evidence of that system change becomes an important part of this stage.

Stage III – Proof and Expansion

This is the advanced stage of a prevention process. It begins when the indicators of success that have been established start to show the impact of the action strategy. Other evidence that this stage has been reached is redirection of community organizations' resources and changes in their organizational designs to incorporate prevention activities. Increased commitment to the concepts and strategies of prevention are in evidence during this stage as new people and organizations move toward joining the effort. Planning of new initiatives to confront other community conditions based upon the original success is characteristic of this stage.

These stages do not necessarily occur in a neat and orderly fashion. A prevention initiative is a dynamic process that builds from the ground up, and a number of things can happen on several fronts. It is useful, however, to be aware of the characteristics of each stage for two reasons. It is important that the people involved are committed to each stage so they do not back off from the task. Being aware of the later stages can encourage them to persist until they get positive results. Secondly, having a sense of where they need to go can help the core group maintain a sense of direction and remain faithful to their task.

SOME RULES-OF-THUMB FOR DEVELOPING PREVENTION STRATEGIES

Because of the complexity of developing prevention strategies and carrying them out effectively, there are many things that can go wrong along the way. Several rules-of-thumb are suggested here in the form of cautions, but they can also guide a group of people as they undertake the difficult task of promoting positive change in their community.

A first rule-of-thumb is suggested by the notion that *issues divide and tasks unite*. If the goals of the prevention effort are clear and if the tasks undertaken to achieve those goals are tangibly related to them, it is often possible to encourage people to work together who might otherwise be at odds ideologically, politically or for other reasons. The process of engaging key allies, if completed sensitively and positively, can bring about new alliances and new experiences in cooperation that are vitally needed for building both short- and long-range prevention capacity in the community.

A second rule-of-thumb is to *use a rifle approach rather than a shotgun approach* in designing prevention strategies. This means that it is more effective to go single-mindedly to the heart of the matter in a limited arena than to scatter the group's resources over a broader and less defined area. A systematic method for beginning with the general and narrowing the focus to a limited, manageable set of goals will be suggested in Chapters IV and V. A general awareness that it is more effective to be successful in a limited area than to dissipate resources in the pursuit of vague goals can encourage the planning group to use its resources to best advantage. This also takes into consideration the idea that positive change in one area of a system can have positive influence in other parts of that system.

A third rule-of-thumb is to *engage only as many people as needed to accomplish the goals of a prevention strategy*. While Quadrant 1 activity does invite participation, it is strategically important not to engage more people than are needed. When people are asked to become a part of something that is important to them, they will want to be kept busy with meaningful tasks. If too many allies are engaged, keeping them busy may become a burden to the leaders and a source of discouragement to those who have been engaged. A well designed prevention strategy will include a clear delineation of the required tasks and the human resources needed to carry out those tasks. Overpopulation of the people resources for the program may be as much of a problem as a lack of needed resource people.

* * *

This chapter has focused upon a number of considerations that are important for building prevention strategies. The task becomes even more challenging as one considers the politics and economics of building prevention capacity. Because of the provocative nature of a prevention approach, it is crucial that those who foster it have a clear and convincing idea of their conceptual base and strategic framework before they get too far from the relative safety of more reactive ways of doing things.   □

chapter 3
The Economics And Politics Of Prevention

Little progress has been made in developing an understanding of prevention. There are many activities that can aptly be described as preventive, both within and outside what we know as the human service system, but we still have not found ways to conceptualize, communicate and make operational a clear and sound approach to prevention that rallies people and invites them to commit their energies and resources to the effort.

Why is this so? The benefits of preventing problems rather than treating them after they occur are so obvious that few would deny them. The situation is, however, quite complex. To place more emphasis on prevention requires coming to grips with the economics and philosophies of the human service system locally, statewide and nationally. That is one major task. There is also a need to examine the values and the politics of the community in which prevention strategies are proposed. That, too, is a difficult challenge. Furthermore, an emphasis on prevention requires changes in attitudes and behavior among many people, including elected officials, appointed policy group members, administrators and service providers. As these changes reach toward the state and federal sources of funds and the legislative requirements that finance and shape many human service activities, similar changes in attitudes, behavior and legislation may be needed at those levels.

In most of the functional areas of human services, a shift in emphasis toward prevention tampers with the economy and the politics of the *status quo*. Practically speaking, this shift in emphasis may require a change in policy, which means an alteration in the thinking among people at the policy level. It may call for a change in organizational design and structure, which means modifying behavior at the administrative level. It may demand a change in skill requirements, which means variations in strategy and behavior at the practitioner level. It may also require changes in the institutions which train and educate decision makers, administrators and practitioners. For all of these changes to occur, a process of reeducation must take place at all of those levels. Finally, and perhaps most importantly, so basic a shift in emphasis requires strong support and involvement among the citizenry whose sanction is necessary for success.

These observations are not intended to discourage; they are meant, rather, to suggest how monumental a task must be undertaken if any real progress is to be made toward developing practical prevention strategies where people live, work, learn, enjoy their leisure and otherwise spend the major portion of their time. It would indeed be unfortunate if the scope of the challenge of discovering the meaning of prevention were underestimated. The forces that militate against an emphasis on prevention are formidable and often come from the very people who might reasonably be expected to provide the leadership toward building prevention capacity. Finding ways to turn these negative factors into positive and practical strategies and resources for prevention is a major part of the challenge.

If these observations "ring true" to any extent, there might be a strong temptation to retreat into cynicism and select a more inviting pastime than trying to promote a positive approach to prevention. After all, anyone with even a little experience in such fields as education, juvenile and criminal justice, mental health, public welfare and other social services, public and private, knows how entrenched and slow to change values and practices can be.

Any attempt either to promote interest in prevention or to implement specific strategies for prevention is an effort to bring about *change*. This includes change in the attitudes and behaviors of individuals and change in the operational patterns of organizations and institutions. To promote these kinds of change requires a clear sense of purpose, a capacity to develop clear goals and objectives, and skills for engaging people in designing and carrying out workable strategies. Because one can reasonably anticipate strong resistance from many directions to the change being sought, a capacity to live with and overcome intense frustration is also useful. This requires a willingness to meet people where they are and to set a pace that is realistic in light of those forces of resistance.

The approach about to be outlined is based upon the idea that *prevention is a process of planned change*. This means that those who would encourage more emphasis on prevention and those who would foster specific prevention efforts are *facilitators of change*, who may find in the following pages some useful ideas about change, change strategies and change agents.

In considering the economics and politics of prevention, it is important to give immediate and forthright attention to the place of human service organizations in a prevention initiative. This is appropriate for several reasons: (1) many of the human, physical and financial resources that can be directed toward prevention can be made available through various human service organizations; (2) people in the community have reasonable and legitimate expectations that human service organizations provide leadership, know-how and other resources for a prevention effort; and (3) the responsibility for prevention in various functional areas of human service is specifically mandated in the charters and enabling legislation of many public and private human service organizations. Generally speaking, prevention is a part of the mission or purpose of many existing organizations, even though these organizations may not have emphasized or developed ways to implement that part of their mission.

In areas where collaborative prevention initiatives have become an obvious and significant part of local or state-level activities, human service personnel have been in the forefront – with clear sanction from their organizations. A common pattern in many communities is that some organizations have given serious consideration to their responsibility for prevention and have made commitments at the policy and staff levels. These organizations either have worked in relative isolation or have attempted to work collaboratively with other organizations with similar interests. This has usually proved to be a difficult and frustrating undertaking because of a number of organizational and system-related restraints.

An examination of some of the forces at work in the human service system and within its various component organizations both helps to build an understanding of some of the positive and negative forces at work and provides a basis for encouraging positive change.

ORGANIZATIONAL LIFESTYLES AND PREVENTION

Many of the resources that might be used for prevention, though by no means all of them, are managed within and offered through the organizations that comprise the human service system. These organizations provide services of various kinds and offer opportunities that are intended to promote the betterment of people and the community.

The human service system in reality belongs to the community, for it is largely financed through a combination of public tax funds, tax deductible contributions, tax-exempt private foundation grants and user fees. Most human service organizations operate under the auspices of units of government or nonprofit corporations which have been exempted from taxation because of their charitable and community service purposes.

The human service system, broadly defined, includes all those service organizations whose efforts focus upon education, law enforcement, justice, corrections, health and mental health, recreation, personal growth and development, employment, income maintenance, protective services, residential placements and other human concerns. As one views the array of human service organizations at the local level and examines the stated purposes of those organizations, certain expectations of them tend to be formed. These expectations may focus upon performance, coordination of effort, relevance of service activities, accountability for the expenditure of public or charitable funds, skill in service delivery and any number of other important matters related to the application of resources to human and community needs. To say the least, the human service system often presents a bewildering picture to a person who is unfamiliar with its complex and, at times, contradictory ways of working. The system itself is frequently the source of intense frustration for those who work within it.

Numerous people who work within the human service system or who relate to it in various ways are expressing increasing dismay about that system and its component parts. This often appears to relate, in part, to discrepancies between the stated purposes of organizations and their performance. To put this another way, the dismay may have to do with the discontinuity between what a person might reasonably expect of an organization and what that person observes about the organization.

This section analyses the politics and economics of prevention relative to *assumptions, expectations, and individual perceptions of reality* that are held within and about human service organizations. The intent is to determine how they might be encouraged to become participants in prevention. Many people have legitimate concerns about human services, their quality and their effectiveness. This includes people who use the services and opportunities provided by the system, people who make decisions about the system, people who work with it professionally or voluntarily, and people who support the system financially through taxes or donations. That probably includes almost everyone.

A complicated relationship might be simply expressed as a process in which:

ASSUMPTIONS *lead to* EXPECTATIONS
followed by PERCEPTIONS OF REALITY.

Generally speaking, if the reality one perceives about an organization measures up to one's expectations of that organization, based upon one's assumptions about the organization, the result will be *satisfaction*. On the other hand, if the reality one perceives does not measure up to one's expectations, the result may be *frustration*, dismay or some other negative response. In the latter situation, one option is to analyze the situation with a view toward mounting a program of planned change in order to bring the reality more in line with the expectations. A possible approach to such an analysis of human service organizations might be to employ the following procedures.

The two lists of assumptions about human service organizations describe differing perceptions about those organizations. The assumptions are consciously overstated to represent opposite ends of a range of possibilities for each set of statements. The first column emanates from what is called the *Service Mode*. The other emanates from what is called the *Survival/Maintenance Mode*. It is suggested that all the statements in the first column be read first, then all the statements in the second column. The next step should be to go back and read the statements paired by being designated by the same numbers to bring out the implications of specific contrasts.

Organizational Lifestyles

The Service Mode

The Survival/Maintenance Mode

1. Human service organizations exist primarily to meet the needs of people and to promote healthy and constructive living conditions in the community.

2. The overriding concern of human service organization policy boards, managers and staff members is to deliver resources (human, physical and financial) to needs.

3. Human service professionals and organizations are willing to take the risks that are necesary to meet human needs and promote positive change in the community.

4. Human service organizations and their staffs are oriented toward seeking those community and organizational changes that will render them increasingly effective to do their service delivery jobs.

5. Human service organizations generally are "out in front" in relation to the community and lead the community toward values and actions that are sensitive to human needs and responsive to those needs.

6. Availability to the clientele of the organization is of primary concern

1. Human service organizations exist primarily to provide jobs for persons who work in them. Human services comprise an important part of the economy of every community.

2. The overriding concern of human service organization policy boards, managers and staff members is to preserve job stability and to maintain the conditions necessary for that stability.

3. Human service professionals and organizations resist taking risks that might jeopardize jobs and organizational stability, even at the expense of more viable and effective services.

4. Human service organizations and their staffs are oriented toward institutional maintenance and resist even those changes that will obviously enable them to improve their services.

5. Human service organizations are reflective of the values of the community and tend to take the shape that will be easily and comfortably tolerated in the community.

6. The convenience of the staff is the primary concern of human service

and human service organizations are oriented toward increasing that availability.

7. Collaboration with other organizations is sought when it will enhance problem solving in the community. Fragmentation of services is seen as detrimental to sound service delivery and resource utilization.

8. Open communication across organizational lines is seen as essential for promoting effective service delivery and resource utilization.

9. A developmental approach to program design that invites a high level of community involvement is essential for promoting a dynamic and relevant service system.

10. Greater emphasis on prevention is seen as healthy for an effective system in the community. Reducing the potential for problems requires change and risk, but this is desirable.

11. Promoting change in those community conditions that cause problems for people is needed and desirable. The behavioral changes to effect this may rest in part with decision makers, human service professionals and other community leaders.

12. Evaluation of organizational effectiveness is seen as essential for improving services. Evaluation is an integral part of program management and necessary for accountability to the community which supports the organization.

organizations and they are oriented toward maintaining practices that serve that convenience.

7. Collaboration and joint approaches to problem solving are resisted because they jeopardize organizational stability and autonomy. Fragmentation is seen as functional for institutional maintenance.

8. Isolation of human service organizations helps to preserve organizational autonomy, so motivation toward communication with other organizations is low.

9. A prescribed approach to program design that allows little community interference is essential for maintaining a stable and controllable service system.

10. Reactive services require little change and risk for human service organizations. Prevention may jeopardize the need for those "safer" service activities, so little emphasis on prevention is seen as desirable.

11. Focus on client change places ownership of "the problem" with the individual and therefore does not require the organization, its leaders and staff or other community leaders to change their behavior.

12. Evaluation of organizational effectiveness is given little emphasis in that it may point up change that is needed or even lead to questions about the validity of the organization's existence.

An examination of these statements reveals that:

A.   Statements 1 and 2 focus on the *Purpose or Mission* of human service organizations.

B.   Statements 3 through 5 focus on the *Quality of Leadership* within and provided in the community by human service organizations.

C.   Statements 6 through 9 focus on the *Quality of Organization/ Community Relationships.*

D.   Statements 10 and 11 focus on *Prevention and Commitment to Positive Community Change.*

E.   Statement 12 focuses on *Program Evaluation.*

A probing discussion of these 12 pairs of statements can help provide a sense of organizational and inter-organizational atmosphere for prevention in a community, at least as that atmosphere relates to the human service system. Use of this process by groups of people in Community Development Workshops has revealed a common pattern of perception. These people tend to have expectations which are close to the Service Mode statements, while their perceptions of reality are closer to the Survival/Maintenance Mode statements.

The discussion of these statements encourages the participants in a workshop to identify those service organizations in the community which are described accurately by the Service Mode statements; to consider the nature of those organizations, their policy groups and their staffs; and to develop a list of some of the qualities and values which identify them with the Service Mode. It similarly encourages participants to develop a list of the qualities and values which tend to promote the Survival/Maintenance Mode within human service organizations. This workshop activity moves then toward a consideration of strategies which can foster movement within the human service organizations of the community toward the Service Mode.

Several kinds of insights can emerge from group discussion of the statements. A common perception is that little interest in prevention is likely to be shown by those organizations which are described by the Survival/ Maintenance Mode. Most groups with which this activity has been conducted conclude that this includes most of the human service organizations of the community, suggesting further the presence of an atmosphere that is at least discouraging, and at worst hostile, toward prevention *within the human service systems* of many communities. This is a condition which, if approached in a systematic manner with care and diplomacy, can be changed.

This raises some questions about the capability within the human service organizations of the community to promote change among themselves. Human service organizations are expected by many to be the change agents of the community. A significant test of their ability to carry this role is their ability to demonstrate positive change strategies applied within the system. If they cannot, it may be necessary to look outside the human service system for leadership for prevention in the community or to foster significant change within human service organizations to prepare them for the leadership task. Realistically, in most communities there may be some human service organizations that are unlikely to become involved in an assertive prevention initiative, but if even a small percentage are ready and willing to move in that direction, these few can become the nucleus of a collaborative prevention effort.

Another important consideration for organizations willing to become involved is that the strategies which can promote positive change within an organization are the same as those which can promote positive change in the community. The organization, then, can use itself as a laboratory for developing the kinds of skills and strategies it will use in the larger community to pursue prevention objectives. This reality will become clearer in the next two chapters, which examine community planning and action strategies. Because these methods are generic, they can be applied in many ways. The admonition, "Physician heal thyself," can be modified to say, "Human service organization change thyself." The capacity for positive community change can be developed by human service organizations if their policy, management and service delivery staff groups are as willing to develop and demonstrate their change skills internally as to practice them externally.

While it is possible to mount a community prevention initiative using only resources outside the human service system, it is best to have at least some of the resources come from that system, where many skills and much knowledge are available and where legislative and other mandates have placed responsibility to provide leadership and other resources needed for the task of prevention.

FORCES THAT SHAPE HUMAN SERVICES

Promoting positive change within human service organizations that will help them participate more fully in prevention activities involves dealing with a number of forces that shape those organizations. Three such forces that are significant factors in considering the politics and economics of prevention will be examined here.

The Inertia of the Survival/Maintenance Mode

The inertia related to the Survival/Maintenance Mode is a powerful force, indeed. Traditions which require little creative thinking, skill building, collaboration with other organizations or personal and organizational risks are found in every community. Organizations characterized by those traditions tend to be so reactive in their operational styles and so caught in deeply entrenched activity traps that it may be unrealistic to expect them to contribute much to a community prevention effort. While this kind of agency should have an opportunity to participate in a prevention initiative, it is probable that others less tradition-bound and more open to exploring new directions will prove to be better allies.

Prescribed Structure Approaches to Program Design

A second kind of force, the *prescribed structure* approach to program design, is institutionalized and dominates much of human services locally and nationally. There are several kinds of prescribed structures, and they tend to predetermine the shape of local human service organizations. These prescriptive forces essentially reside outside the community where the organization they have shaped exists. If they are not understood, these forces will militate against an emphasis on prevention because, although they are shaped with the best of intentions and may in fact promote good results, they can also serve to inhibit a prevention initiative.

Four important prescribed forces are (1) federal and state legislation, (2) funding mandates and guidelines, (3) national affiliations and (4) professional education. Some important questions to ask in relation to these forces are:

- Do they tend to discourage local participation in and ownership of local program design processes?

- Do they pre-empt the way organizational resources will be used so creative prevention activities are discouraged?

- Do they tend to usher people into activity traps, leading them to such an emphasis on predetermined, structured activity that they do not attend to the essential elements of change processes?

- Are the people who shape these forces really knowledgeable of local conditions, needs and opportunity patterns?

- Is there sufficient interaction between local people and those who shape these strong prescribed forces so that creative organizational designs can result?

Prescribed structures tend to be authoritarian in nature. They are "from the top down." They tend to say, at least in relation to legislation and funding mandates and guidelines, "In order to receive these funds you must include these specific program components." As an example, several years ago a state agency, through which federal "delinquency prevention" funds passed, required that *at least 50% of the referrals taken had to come from police sources.* This meant that in order to receive these "prevention" funds, the organization had to take referrals of young people apprehended by the police, a Quadrant 4 remedial task. This kind of funding guideline preempted the "prevention" programs in such a way that little experimentation in the prevention arenas was possible.

Other local agencies which receive governmental funding, notably those which work in the mental health and public welfare areas, are bound by rather specific funding guidelines. Ironically, these requirements have assured certain services to geographical areas where they otherwise might not have been offered, while at the same time possibly creating some political realities discouraging to prevention activity.

National affiliations lend strength to local programs and help to promote standards of practice that would be difficult to achieve by organizations on their own. These same affiliations, however, at times lead local organizations into designs that were shaped by people who lived in other decades and who were far removed from the local community where the organization exists. Strong prescriptive forces at work within these organizations tend to discourage assertive efforts to address specialized local needs and conditions in a preventive manner. Some of these national organizations, many of which are funded through local United Ways, encourage their local affiliates to become more responsive to local conditions, however, and provide technical assistance that supports more creative local programming. They have recognized that a prescribed structure may lead to stereotyped and unimaginative organizational designs.

The relationship of professional education to local program design is complex. The connection between theory and practice in human services is often obscure, and there is a continuing concern about the manner in which higher education prepares people to practice. The kinds of influence that various types of professional training have on the shape of programs that deliver services at the community level should be examined. For example, a school of social work that prepares a social caseworker for the field of practice is both influenced by and influences service patterns in the community. When large numbers of social caseworkers are trained in a similar manner by several schools of social work, the shape of local programs will of course be influenced as those professionals assume line and administrative positions in the field. At the same time, those same people receive part of their training during student internships in local agencies and are thereby strongly influenced by the ways those organizations work.

The repetitious patterns which exist in both courses of professional education and the service organizations in which professionals work suggest that strong prescriptive forces are at work. This may be explained in part by the sense of security, both personal and organizational, which cultural patterns provide. It may result, too, from the influence that the "technology" of a particular field of service, such as mental health or education, has on both training for a profession and the practice of it.

The important point here is that if change is to occur within an organization or group of organizations that will encourage effective involvement in a community prevention activity, the nature of these complex forces must be understood. Indeed, a part of the long range strategy for discovering the meaning of prevention must be focused upon encouraging educational institutions which train professionals to take prevention more seriously. A balance among the four arenas of human service activity within human services depends upon having professional education assume a responsible role. Since the meaning of prevention usually is discovered in the local community, those who work in prevention need to encourage their local citizens to make demands upon higher education institutions to assume that role.

The prescriptive forces mentioned share several relevant characteristics with other prescribed structures which strongly shape local service organizations and the effectiveness of prevention initiatives. They most often are *outside forces* which may inhibit local initiative and responsibility. This creates problems around developing local ownership. Because it takes several years for the prescriptive force to take shape and be felt in the local community, it is probable that the force itself is at least several years behind the community. This time lag between service design and implementation in the community may render the resulting service less than relevant to today's conditions. Prescriptive forces by their very nature are based on yesterday's assessment of yesterday's needs. This is not to say that they cannot and do not make positive contributions to the community. It does clearly suggest, though, that if human service resources are to be used wisely, the design processes which shape them must remain current with the conditions they address. Sound management of resources, whether in the business or the human service sector, requires a continuing reexamination of objectives as they relate to community conditions. This may, and usually does, involve revision of those objectives to adjust to changing times. *Prescriptive forces tend to militate against dynamic resource management.*

Developmental Process Approaches to Program Design

Another kind of force that shapes local human services provides a corrective to the negative aspects of the prescriptive forces that so dominate the human service systems of most communities. This is the *developmental process* approach. In contrast to the prescribed structure, the developmental process works "from the ground up." It begins with a recognition of a condition that needs to be addressed (Condition A), analyzes and describes that condition, realistically determines what a more desirable condition would be (Condition B), and proceeds to shape a change strategy that is capable of dealing effectively with that condition in a positive way.

A well designed and managed developmental process can overcome some of the problems inherent in the prescribed structure approach. It can also address the problems of inertia related to the Survival/Maintenance Mode. A developmental process builds around the active concerns of people as they decide they want to bring about change of some kind. This might be a crisis-oriented effort, or it might emanate from a desire to improve a particular situation. It can focus on individual change or changes in conditions. In other words, just as with programs designed through the prescribed structure approach, human service activities in each of the four arenas can be designed through a developmental process.

A strategy designed within the community through a developmental process has high potential for a sense of *local ownership* to develop around it. The strategy is designed by people who will be using it, whose motivation comes from a desire to produce the sought-for change. This kind of participation and ownership can be a powerful force to assure that the strategy is implemented and achieves the intended results.

The strategies for prevention suggested throughout this book are essentially community development (Quadrant 1) strategies and have been designed through this kind of developmental process. The following story helps to illustrate the dynamics of a developmental process.

A Story of Two Communities

The people of Urbansville were concerned about various problems facing young people in their community. A small group of youths and adults gathered to develop some plans. They compared their own ideas and impressions, and they talked with numerous others in the community. They also compiled some specific information that reflected conditions of young people (Condition A). After satisfying themselves that they had built a good understanding of the youth situation, they began to consider what kind of community they wanted for young people to grow up in (Condition B). Then they began to organize a program designed around the results of their hard work. They experimented as they went. Interest was high and increasing numbers of people became involved – *youths and adults working together*. Local resources, financial and otherwise, were gathered and were supplemented by a grant of federal money.

After two years and much learning, interest was still high and growing, for the people of Urbansville were seeing that their program was working to their satisfaction. Indeed, it was accomplishing what they wanted it to. Changes were occurring in the community, fewer young people were getting referred to the court, and the forces for positive action were growing stronger.

The program began to attract attention outside Urbansville, and the federal funding source began saying, with much pride, "Look what we're doing!" A description was written in a national publication, and their program was singled out statewide for special recognition.

The people of Urbansvile appreciated this confirmation of their good work, but they didn't let it distract them. They continued to work at the tasks of improving their program and experimenting with new ways to keep people involved and working together to create better conditions for young people.

When the federal grant ran out, the people of Urbansville raised more money in the community to keep things moving. They knew what their program was all about and they would not let anything happen to endanger it.

About that time some people from Copystown decided they, too, were concerned about youth problems. The funding source said it would give money to support programs like the one in Urbansville because it was so successful. It had become "the model." Before writing their proposal for funds, some people from Copystown went to visit Urbansville. They borrowed a copy of the organization chart of the Urbansville program and some other descriptive materials. Within two months they organized and "installed" a program "just like" the one in Urbansville.

The people of Copystown continued to operate their program, but somehow it did not seem to work as well as the one in Urbansville. It did not have the excitement or hold the people's interest as well as the original version.

After three years the people of Copystown were notified by the funding source that their grant had run out and they would have to look elsewhere for funds. They had been told this much earlier, but they figured they could do something about it later. Now the time had come, and for some reason the community did not seem interested in providing local support. The people of Copystown scratched their heads and wondered, "Urbansville did it. Why couldn't we?"

Working Developmentally in a Highly Prescribed World

While generalizations may not fit every specific situatuion, they do have value to the task of clarifying the place of prevention in the broader picture of human services. Generally speaking, the human service system in most communities is shaped for the most part by prescribed forces, and the Survival/Maintenance Mode is alive, well and actively at work within most human service organizations. While such organizations should not be seen as the only prevention resources, much of value to a prevention initiative resides within or can be developed within them. This includes human, physical and financial resources. Strategies for prevention should include engaging those resources in positive ways at the same time other community resources are recruited and involved.

Developmental processes are always to some extent at work within, through and around prescribed structures. Those who promote prevention strategies in the community do well to accept the challenge to learn how to engage others in building from the ground up. Allies in this process will include those who work within the highly prescribed organizations of the community, including organizations which provide remedial services. Indeed, such persons may take the initiative and provide leadership for prevention.

Well designed prevention strategies can have positive impact on service organizations which might be heavily committed to remedial activity. The second stage of a prevention process, described in Chapter II, suggests that such influence is evidence that prevention strategies are taking hold. When these organizations volunteer staff time for prevention initiatives, rewrite job descriptions to incorporate Quadrant 1 and Quadrant 2 activity and refocus some of their programs in a more preventive direction, this impact is occurring.

Prevention initiatives that are developmental and proactive must intrude upon a service system and other community institutions that are essentially prescribed and reactive. It is not surprising that prevention has made so little headway, and it is probable that it will continue to have an uphill battle. But prevention makes sense, and those who will foster an interest in it will make progress by presenting their case with persuasive clarity. In times of strongly conservative political trends, budgetary concerns may lead to cutbacks of governmental support for human service programs. On the surface, reduced funding for social programs would appear to make an emphasis on prevention even more difficult to achieve. This need not be the case. Those who promote prevention as a potentially more cost-effective way to confront long-standing community problems have a strong position. The question is how to encourage thoughtful community leaders to explore and support more effective, cost-saving approaches to dealing with community problems. How can this be accomplished in a manner that does not threaten existing service organizations, but rather builds on their available knowledge and other strengths?

DOES YOUR COMMUNITY HAVE A WELL-DEFINED PREVENTION POLICY?

A useful and interesting project for those who would become assertive in promoting prevention focuses upon the place of prevention in shaping policies that give direction to program design and resource allocation decisions. This project could be carried out efficiently by four or five knowledgeable people in a two- or three-week period. It can start with a simple listing of all of the major decision-making groups that have some authority over organizations which might reasonably be expected to provide leadership for prevention.

After this list is completed, the group might quickly review, based upon its members' current knowledge, the level of understanding various members of those policy groups have of prevention and their commitment to it. This review might include noting any recent decisions these groups have made that indicated some interest in or support of prevention.

A next step is to list specific members of these decision making groups who can be contacted by phone or face-to-face interview to talk about their understanding of prevention and opinions about it. Doing this on a selective basis (eight or 10 such contacts should be enough) should result in enough information to define rather clearly where prevention stands with the policy makers of the community.

Such groups as the school board, the city council, the United Way board of directors executive committee and the policy groups of three or four of the major private human service agencies of the community might be invited to share in this simple procedure that should reveal whether or not the community has a clearly defined prevention policy.

The shaping of policy, by its very nature, is a political process. It is unlikely that prevention will make much headway in any of the human service organizations unless some attention is given to the changing of some of the policies that shape program design and determine resource allocations. This is not to say that important steps cannot be taken in the interest of prevention without dealing with policy formation, but a serious effort to promote prevention will need to deal with policy making and policy groups.

An important distinction is that between *policy* and *program*. Policy is defined as "a definite course or method of action selected from among alternatives and in light of given conditions to guide and determine present and future decisions."[4] Program includes a set of specific activities carried out to achieve organizational goals. Policy provides a set of operational principles in light of which program decisions can be made.

If a policy group were to consider and adopt a *prevention policy*, some operational principles would be available to guide program decisions. This could help to avoid the need continually to make reactive decisions under the pressure of crisis or near-crisis situations. A prevention policy would encourage both policy groups and program staff people to think more *proactively* about how positive conditions which promote the well-being of people can be created.

A method for assisting a group of people to make this distinction between policy and program and to think about its implications for their community is a simulation activity that is used in the Community Development Workshop. This simulation, entitled "Developing a Community Youth Policy," engages the participants in interaction with one another in an effort to shape a policy to guide decisions about the allocation of resources that affect the young people of the community. The guidelines for this simple but highly engaging activity are as follows:

The Situation

The city council, in a recent study session, was urged to develop some new policies to determine their funding allocations for youth programs. The director of Youth Advocates, Inc., a nonprofit organization with an active interest in the prevention of youth problems, made a strong plea to the council for more emphasis on positive youth development, youth involvement and prevention. This interested most of the council members, and a decision was made to hold an open community meeting to get more information and ideas as a step toward adopting a statement of youth policy.

The meeting has been announced, and various groups of people plan to attend to present their viewpoints.

The Task

The following groups of people attend the meeting. Workshop participants are randomly assigned roles they will play in the simulation.

A. The City Council

With one member of the council serving as mayor, this group listens as a panel to the ideas of the other groups. Each member of the council has a point of view and tries to represent his or her constituents.

B. Youth Advocates Staff and Board

As members of the group which stimulated the meeting with the council, these individuals see themselves as having an educational role to promote interest in prevention and a facilitating role to encourage community involvement.

C. The PTA Executive Committee

This group is made up of PTA parents who represent the schools in various neighborhoods throughout the city.

D. The Interagency Council

This group is made up of human service professionals who work in a broad range of youth serving organizations. They are concerned about interagency coordination and greater awareness of the human service resources of the community.

E. The United Way Executive Committee

These high-level business executives serve on the United Way board of directors. They make decisions about the distribution of funds donated by the United Way campaign.

F. The Juvenile Law Enforcement Officers Association

Juvenile officers from various law enforcement agencies in the metropolitan area have formed this group. They have been organized for several years and have been vocal advocates for their interests.

G. The Central City Neighborhood Residents Association

This group is made up of residents of several housing projects in the inner city who have organized around concerns about housing, transportation, crime, police/community relations, welfare rights, recreation facilities and other matters.

H. Young People

This is a diverse group of young people. Some represent organized youth groups while others just come to express themselves.

The various groups meet separately at first for a specific period of time (20 minutes) to determine how they will participate in the public meeting. It is important that a wide variety of attitudes, opinions and values are expressed at the meeting. Also, it is important that each group considers what it can offer in helping to develop a sound youth policy for the city.

A second period of time is designated (40 minutes) for interaction among the groups to consider the possibility of alliances that will be useful in shaping new policy.

The city council then conducts a public meeting. (This lasts about an hour and 15 minutes.) Each of the groups comes prepared, through a spokesperson, to make a brief presentation (five minutes or less) about what it thinks should be included in the policy. The mayor chairs the meeting.

General discussion regarding the issues raised follows.

The Objective

The objective of the simulation is to examine the various forces at work in the community as people represent different vested interests to see if some agreement on an approach to developing a youth policy can begin to emerge.

The group is encouraged to move toward finding a clear sense of direction in a manner that is realistic for a first meeting. Positive behaviors can be tested as participants carry their roles. Creative efforts at collaboration can be tried as people with different vested interests and opinions represent themselves and their constituents. The group is encouraged to use the most effective problem solving and decision making strategies and techniques they have at their disposal.

There are two different ways this workshop activity can be staged. One is to ask the participants to act out the ways they think people in the various roles would act in reality, with a focus on examining some of the natural roadblocks and stereotyped kinds of thinking and behaving that need to be faced and dealt with in developing policy.

Another approach is to ask the participants to come to the meeting intent on finding effective and imaginative ways to working out a comprehensive youth policy that emphasizes prevention. This approach gives the participants an opportunity to experiment with some positive, and perhaps new, behavior focused on making progress.

The thoughtful use of this experiential activity can encourage a community group to take some assertive action in the interest of clarifying prevention policy. The director of the Office of Youth Services in the city of Manchester, New Hampshire, has reported the outcome of his community's using this process:

> On September 2, 1980 the Manchester, New Hampshire Board of Mayor and Aldermen unanimously adopted a Youth Policy, concluding more than a year's efforts by numerous Manchester adults and young people. The adoption defined where the community stood in its efforts to assist its young people in becoming responsible community members and charted the direction in which the community wanted to move in that continuing effort.[5]

In this example a significant number of people in a city have gone through a democratic, participatory process to shape a comprehensive policy through which decisions can be made and prevention can assume its place along with other human service considerations.

When people are helped to experience what it means to make policy and how a policy decision may affect the entire community, it becomes possible to encourage them to begin to develop an assertive approach to shaping policy measures they see as positive. This is needed if prevention is to gain consideration as an important force for positive community change.

CONDUCTING A COMMUNITY PREVENTION INVENTORY

As has been suggested, in order to bring about planned change, it is useful to know where one is beginning (Condition A). Those interested in fostering more emphasis on prevention can undertake a community prevention inventory to gain an accurate picture of the current status of prevention from a political and economic perspective. Much of the information that relates to the items below will be readily available to people who know the community well, or they will know where it can be obtained. Some items may have to be estimated.

An Outline for a Community Prevention Inventory

The purpose of this outline is to provide a systematic approach to gaining a specific understanding of the current "state of the art" of prevention in the community that can then be used to plan action strategies for increasing the interest in and capacity for prevention in the future.

Three steps are suggested. The first is to describe the current condition using the areas suggested by the outline. The second is to describe a new set of conditions to be achieved one year hence in relation to a stronger, more desirable and realistic emphasis on prevention. The third step is to prepare a set of recommendations which will shape a program of planned change toward more effective prevention efforts.

Focal Areas for the Prevention Inventory:

A. Definitions and concepts of prevention currently in use.

B. The relative amount of emphasis given to prevention.

C. Existing policy supporting prevention.

D. The amount of youth involvement and adult non-professional citizen involvement in current prevention activities.

E. Examples of specific strategies being used.

F. A description of the current emphasis on evaluation of prevention activities.

G. A description of any interagency, interorganization, intergovernment collaboration in progress that supports prevention. Also any collaboration between functional areas (examples are education, juvenile justice, recreation, mental health, etc.)

H. Specific state/local relationships supporting prevention.
I. Specific training/technical assistance available to support prevention.
J. Earmarked funding available for prevention.
K. Names of specific key people providing leadership for prevention. (List their positions.)
L. A description of the level of interest in seeing prevention get more emphasis. (Illustrate with examples.)

After the inventory is completed, it should be possible to shape some realistic goals to work on during the coming year and some practical recommendations around which a program to promote specific changes can be designed.

The use of this inventory and the development of strategies for change based upon it constitute human service activity in the community development (Quadrant 1) arena. Pursuing this process can provide a way of gauging the responsiveness of the human service system of the community and the potential for leadership for assertive prevention activity.

This inventory can also be used at the state level as a step toward building a statewide support system for prevention, a matter that is addressed in Chapter VII.

Those who commit themselves to promoting prevention in their community should be aware that as this kind of change process is undertaken conditions in the community that have a direct relationship to the symptoms to be prevented already are being addressed. This will become more apparent in the next chapter as we focus on ways of viewing the community from a prevention perspective.

A practical approach to understanding and confronting the political and economic aspects of prevention will inevitably become a part of the process of discovering the meaning of prevention. While this reality might tend to discourage or even frighten some people it can also become one of the more enjoyable and exciting aspects of the venture. A more positive attitude can be developed toward the political and economic aspects of community change when those involved discover that the pursuit of positive goals can bring people together in a joint endeavor. At best, building a better community through positive prevention strategies is an engaging activity that has many positive rewards for those involved. ☐

chapter 4
Viewing The Community From A Prevention Perspective

Any assertive approach to discovering the meaning of prevention will at some point move out of the realm of general discussion and into the realm of specific, targeted action directed toward attaining tangible results. This movement must happen in the midst of the economic and political realities explored in the last chapter. This challenging task requires a set of strategies that is capable of assisting those involved in determining their direction, setting priorities, designing an action plan, engaging needed allies, generating resources, overcoming any obstacles and gauging their progress. These requirements are the focus of this and the next two chapters.

The first stage of a well designed prevention initiative as described in Chapter II focuses upon "orientation, training and planning." Getting started is a practical task that has presented many community groups with insurmountable obstacles. The approach suggested here builds upon the inevitable diversity of opinion that exists among those who need to be involved. When one considers the decision makers, the professionals, the private citizens (both youth and adult) and other identifiable groups of people who might participate, the question immediately arises as to how these diverse persons can be encouraged to work together in a cooperative manner. One approach might be to bring together a group of likeminded people, to avoid the confusion that is likely to result. Through the use of an action training strategy such as the Community Development Workshop, though, it is possible to create a situation that capitalizes upon diverse opinions in a highly structured process that leads those involved from the general to the specific in a productive manner.

The ideas, strategies and activities described in this chapter help participants in the prevention effort to view their community from a prevention perspective. This includes identifying some starting points, and this can be done in a way that helps the participants explore the differences in the perspectives of Quadrant 1 and Quadrant 4.

An important value that underlies the idea of gathering people with potentially differing points of view is that everyone involved is a *resource person*. If the mayor of the city is involved, his or her opinion and experience is of no more or less value than that of a delinquent young person who might also be involved. Each perspective contributes to the building of an action plan that can have broad ownership among people in the community. Creating a situation in which two such persons are working together to discover effective prevention strategies can provide each with a new learning experience that can have profound impact upon community conditions. The process of discovery is enriched through the diversity of perspective as people explore concepts, strategies, tools and skills for prevention.

The first of the three essential ingredients of a change process is knowing where one is (Condition A). A useful initial activity in a Community Development Workshop, or in any attempt to initiate a prevention strategy, is to identify those factors which are contributing to the symptoms one wishes to prevent. It is often said, "We know what the problems are. We have studied them extensively. Let's get on with the action!" If this is true, the possibilities for moving through this stage of the process rather efficiently are great. It would be a real disservice to those involved and to the community, however, if impatience were to deter the participants from putting some basic building blocks into place. Recognition of a problem never has assured that something will be done about it.

An insight that deserves attention is that *the approach to analyzing a problem can become a part of the solution, particularly if people who can exercise some control over the conditions which need to be changed become involved in a positive and constructive manner.* As an example, let us say that there is concern about excessive vandalism that is occurring in a section of the city. In order to seek a preventive solution to this problem, a Community Development Workshop is organized and a group of 25 carefully selected people having a variety of perspectives are invited to attend. As these people consider the nature of the conditions that appear to contribute to the problem, they begin to see specific ways those conditions can be changed. Importantly, they also begin to see how particular people, including themselves, can influence or exercise control over certain aspects of those conditions. Thus they discover that their approach to analyzing the problem becomes a significant part of the solution.

Another point to be drawn from this example is that action training can be both a *means* of helping people develop specific skills for prevention, and a *method* for promoting a particular change in the community. In this sense, training is clearly seen as a direct service option for prevention, as indicated in Chapter II.

Focusing on conditions allows the group of diverse people to deal with community realities without pointing accusing fingers of blame at individuals. The sections of this chapter present specific approaches to viewing the community from a prevention perspective. These are not just additional ways of "studying the problem." As strategies for encouraging a prevention perspective they are strategies for change which provide first steps toward substantial prevention action.

THE YOUTH OPPORTUNITY PLANNING PROCESS (Parts I and II)

The development of effective prevention strategies requires that people with diverse opinions, perspectives and experiences pool their various ideas and shape them into specific and tangible work plans that, when carried out, achieve desirable results.

For the past several years Associates for Youth Development, Inc. has been involved in the development of an approach to using the insights of people systematically within a community to shape a preventive strategy. While this effort has been directed toward positive *youth* development, the methods described below can be focused upon other concerns as well.

This three part process is called *The Youth Opportunity Planning Process*. It is based upon several assumptions about people, their resources and their need for specific procedures for using those resources. These include the assumptions that (1) out of their own experience people have insights that can be put to positive use; (2) most people fail to use these insights because they lack a way to combine them constructively with the insights of others; (3) people often follow paths that are, in fact, *in conflict with their own beliefs*; and (4) if people can become aware of these conflicts, they can mobilize their insights and energies more productively and with a clear sense of direction. This process is best used with a group of concerned individuals in a workshop setting.

Parts I and II of the Youth Opportunity Planning Process relate to problem identification and analysis; Part III is presented in the next chapter and is related to action planning. The total process is as follows:

The Youth Opportunity Planning Process (YOPP)

Part I – The Identification of Contributing Factors

Part I engages the participants in identifying those factors in their community which they believe contribute to problems young people experience. Each factor is described in a brief sentence and discussed enough so all participants agree on its meaning. The factors are then ranked in order of their importance and each receives a numerical value which indicates its relative importance. Discussion is quite general at this stage.

Part II – Analysis of the Factors

In Part II the factors are analyzed as they relate to several questions. The group's responses to these questions are discussed, analyzed and fed back to the group. The discussion becomes increasingly specific at this stage. Specific information that is useful for planning purposes results from this analysis.

Part III – Application of the Factors for Action Planning

Part III focuses quite specifically on what is happening in relation to each factor in the community and provides a clear framework for developing short- and long-range strategies for doing something about each of the selected factors in the community.

The step-by-step procedure of the YOPP assists the participants in moving from the general to the specific as they consider their community. The process can be used in a relatively short period of time, so it is quite efficient. If skillfully conducted it can help to promote good communication and better awareness within the group. When it is focused upon youth concerns it is particularly valuable as a means of promoting productive and serious working relationships among young people and adults.

The first two parts of the YOPP are described in some detail because they illustrate a developmental process through which a group of people can pool their diverse insights and move systematically toward a specific, targeted action plan. The experience of using the procedure confronts some of the realities of the community as the participants identify them, as shown in the discussion below.

Using Part I of the YOPP – The Identification of Contributing Factors

The participants are organized into several small work groups of five to seven persons, with each small group having a diverse mix of people. Each work group then develops a list of several brief statements which describe some of the factors its members believe contribute to the problems of young people in their community. Without going into too much detail, the groups should discuss each factor sufficiently to clarify what it means.

Since the purpose of this first part is to identify in a very general manner important contributing factors, the statements are brief (a dozen words or less), and they should be distinct from one another. That is, it is useful to have only one statement that points in a particular direction, even though the realities the factor identifies may be quite complex. For example, if the wide range of matters related to the family that might contribute to youth problems are seen as important, one summary statement pointing to the family will serve as a "direction pointer" for the purposes of the YOPP. The following guide is used to help the groups shape their statements:

Questions to Ask of Each Factor

1. Is it specific enough to "get a handle" on?
2. Is it worded in a way that is practical for planning and action purposes?
3. It is written in simple and understandable language?

After the small groups have worked on their statements for about 20 minutes all their ideas are contributed to the compilation of a total group list by the reassembled workshop participants. Similarities in statements are considered as each group presents its list and general discussion among the participants helps to negotiate statements that are understood and acceptable to the entire group. As each statement is agreed upon, it is added to a working list of the statements.

Several things happen in this first stage of the YOPP, and it is useful to discuss them within the group. First, *the diverse opinions of the group members emerge.* The value of the diversity is demonstrated quite clearly. For example, a young person recently released from a correctional school will join in the discussion from a vantage point different from that of a high school principal, a juvenile court judge or the parents of an achieving, non-delinquent young person. Each of these opinions can be valued and used to benefit the process.

Second, *as contributions from the different groups are presented, negotiated and clarified it will become apparent that clear communication of ideas is often difficult to achieve.* Just as this discussion helps to clarify the statements, it also illlustrates an important roadblock to developing prevention capacity. For example, if sub-groups of people in the workshop have differing assumptions or definitions of terms and these are not resolved, communication problems can result. A skilled facilitator can encourage the group to persist through this task, which might otherwise become tedious and inefficient.

Third, *it is easy for counterproductive competition to develop among the small work groups as statements are presented and negotiated.* This tends to fragment the group's resources and inhibits the completion of the task.

In a real sense, the people participating in this process become the community in microcosm and experience both the problems and the possibilities that exist in the larger community. This becomes part of the instructive value of the YOPP, particularly as members of the group see that they can move through and beyond some of the usual roadblocks to constructive action. As people develop and adopt the norms of tolerance of diverse opinions, clear communication, listening to others' points of view and a cooperative approach through which all persons emerge as "winners," they will experience greater success in positive collaboration.

When at least 10 statements that meet the suggested criteria have been developed and the group is satisfied that it has a good, comprehensive working list, then the members, individually and without further discussion, rank the factors in priority order, selecting the 10 factors each believes to be the most important. After each person has completed this task, the rankings become the focus of small group discussion as the results are tabulated and members listen to each other's responses and interact about the reasons for their selections. The results of these steps are fed back to the total group to be used for Part II of the YOPP.

An example of the results of Part I of the YOPP, as completed by people from a southeastern community, appears below. These results were selected because they are typical in several important respects. The numbers after each statement indicate the total points given the factor by the workshop participants and reflect the relative importance of each factor as seen by the group members collectively. (Twenty-three persons participated in developing this list, making possible a total of 230 points for any factor.)

1. Poor parenting and broken family ties.   (224)

2. Schools fail to meet the student's needs.   (163)

3. Negative peer pressure.   (150)

4. Lack of economic, physiological and psychological stability.   (138)

5. Lack of employment and vocational training and outdated child labor laws.   (110)   (Tie)

6. Easy access to drugs and alcohol.   (110)   (Tie)

7. Inadequacies of the juvenile justice system.   (95)

8. Attitudes of the community as a whole toward the juvenile delinquency problem.   (89)

9. Lack of youth involvement in community planning.   (82)

10. Inadequate recreational opportunities.   (77)

The list of factors is typical in several respects of those developed by groups with which this process has been conducted. Concern about the home and family is usually first on the list and more often than not is significantly ahead of the second item, as in this example. The institutional areas of family, school, the economy, recreation and juvenile justice are typically addressed. This group showed some bias regarding juvenile justice in its list, which reflects the fact that most of the members work in that functional area.

The lists of factors prepared by various groups, whether urban or rural and regardless of cultural or ethnic makeup, are remarkably similar. This kind of result tends to underscore the idea that communities experience very similar patterns and that people tend to view them in similar ways. This has some important implications for the design of prevention efforts. A significant trend that has emerged from use of this procedure is that people who work in different functional areas (education, mental health, juvenile justice, recreation, family service, etc.) tend to develop similar lists, suggesting that they perceive the factors which promote the symptoms their part of the human service system addresses to be common factors. While the fragmentation and functional divisions that exist in remedial work may have some rationale, this awareness suggests that collaboration in the interests of prevention among functional service areas is needed.

If the factors which promote the symptoms one wishes to prevent tend to promote a diversity of symptoms, then the failure to develop comprehensive approaches in the community to address these factors borders on being irresponsible on the part of decision makers, service providers and interested citizens. We have seen, though, that the economics and the politics of the community, particularly those that relate to the human service system, tend to militate against collaboration across functional and organizational lines. When people from the various functional areas participate in the YOPP it is possible to lay the groundwork for a cooperative prevention effort. Indeed, the YOPP has been designed to foster this kind of collaboration.

While the use of the YOPP at this general first stage produces some important insights, the results of the second stage are even more impressive.

Using Part II of the YOPP –
Analysis of the Factors

The second part of the YOPP encourages the participants to consider the nature of the factors they have identified in terms of how resources are currently being used in relation to them and how they might be best approached with prevention in mind. The 10 factors selected in Part I are subjected to analysis through the use of several questions. The first six of these questions are related to four scales, and participants record their responses on a scale of 1-9. The opinions of the entire group can then be tabulated numerically.

Question A – The Individual/Situational Scale. A key consideration in understanding a problem and potential ways to prevent it is to determine the nature of the factors contributing to the difficulty and their relation to the individual experiencing the difficulty. Question A has to do with the extent to which an individual young person can control a particular factor:

Is this factor something an individual young person can exercise control over, or is it a situational phenomenon that is beyond the control of the individual?

The scale of 9 to be used for response is as follows:

1	2	3	4	5	6	7	8	9
Total control by individual			Combination of individual and situational				Totally situational	

If the factor is seen as being totally within the control of a young person, the response should be a 1. If the factor is seen as totally situational and beyond the control of the individual young person, the response should be a 9. If it is seen as a combination of both, the appropriate number somewhere between should be selected. This question is asked about each of the 10 factors and the response is recorded on a response form by each participant.

Question B – The Youth Behavior/Adult Behavior Scale. In order to have the greatest possible effect on contributing factors, it is important to use strategies that are planned to affect behavior in the most useful manner. Question B attempts to identify those persons whose behavior, if changed, could have the most effect on the factor:

In order to do something about this factor, will your strategies emphasize trying to change the behavior of a young person or group of young people, or will they emphasize trying to change the behavior of an adult or group of adults?

The response to this question is made by selecting a point on the following scale:

1	2	3	4	5	6	7	8	9

Youth behavior change   Combination of youth and adult behavior change   Adult behavior change

If the preferred strategy totally emphasizes youth behavior change, the responses will be a 1. If the emphasis is totally on adult behavior change, a 9 is used. Again, a combination of youth and adult behavior change calls for an appropriate response between the extremes. This question is asked relative to all 10 factors and the responses are recorded.

Question C – The Remediation/Prevention Scale. In order to plan sound and effective change strategies it is important to have a clear sense of purpose in mind from the beginning. Question C has to do with the purpose of the change strategies that are preferred in relation to each factor:

In order to plan sound strategy to deal with this factor, will your primary purpose to be remedy the effects of the factor or will it be to have preventive impact on the factor?

The scale for this question is as follows:

1	2	3	4	5	6	7	8	9

Remedial strategy   Combination of remedial and preventive   Preventive strategy

Again, the participants register their opinions on the scale for each of the 10 factors.

Question D – Individual Change/Condition Change Scale. It is important in planning change to have clearly in mind what the focus of the change effort is going to be. Question D relates to the focus of the change strategy for each factor:

Will your strategies for this factor focus primarily on changing individuals or will they focus on changing conditions that affect people?

The responses are given on the scale as follows:

1	2	3	4	5	6	7	8	9
Focus on individual change			Combination of change of individuals and conditions				Focus on change in conditions	

These questions encourage the participants to think seriously about the factors they have identified as being significant in the lives of young people. The responses they give are based upon their opinions about those factors and how they think they should be viewed.

It will be noted that the "C" and "D" questions deal with the *purpose* and *focus* of preferred strategies in relation to these 10 factors, and these two considerations relate to the Purpose Continuum and the Focus Continuum of the "Arenas of Human Service Activity." It becomes possible, then, to graphically display the responses of the group in a way that reveals their preferences for the kinds of service activities they believe can best address these important contributing factors.

After workshop participants have responded to the "C" and "D" questions in a way that reflects their *preferences* related to the purpose and focus of strategies for dealing with the factors, they are then asked to respond to the "C" and "D" questions again in relation to *how they think the resources of their community are currently being used to deal with these factors*. This encourages the participants to consider the existing conditions (Condition A) of service delivery related to the factors, while the first response to the "C" and "D" questions reflected opinions about the *desired* conditions for service delivery (Condition B).

With this information in hand from the group, a summary of its members' beliefs about these factors can be presented as in Figure 2. The next step is to examine the community's handling of the situation as described by the answers to the six questions. The examination begins with a seventh question. *How is the community dealing with these factors at present?*

This question of Part II of the YOPP uses a column on the response form that is headed by a check mark. After having studied each of the factors carefully in relation to the first six questions, the group members are asked to put a check mark by each factor which they believe is *being approached in their community in a planned and systematic manner.* This task probes further into the perspectives of the group members, revealing how they view the way resources are currently being used in the community and the extent to which they see a collaborative effort under way to deal with these important matters.

As can be seen in the check mark column of Figure 2, the example group perceived very little in their community in the way of collaborative work done about their selected factors. Group averages most frequently fall between one and two check marks per person. Experience with this procedure establishes that *in most communities people perceive very little planned and systematic action taking place to confront those factors which they believe to be contributing to the problems of people.*

Some useful and immediate tabulation of the check mark column can be completed by asking group members how many check marks were given to each factor. In Figure 2, for example, the group overwhelmingly agreed that "poor parenting and broken family ties" was the most important factor. It received 224 out of a possible 230 points in the ranking. Yet only one person in the group perceived that this important factor was being dealt with in a planned and systematic manner. When one thinks about it, there are probably more organizational resources focused upon strengthening family life than any other important aspect of human life, but few communities address it comprehensively and in a coordinated fashion.

The use of the check mark column alone begins to establish a perception within the participant group that prevention is often given little value in the community by governmental units or by human service policy groups, public or private. It may be recognized that resources are being directed toward each of these areas of concern, but the important thing is that such resources are not working together in a planned and systematic manner. The perceptions of the group in relation to the Survival/Maintenance Mode also add to this picture of the manner in which resources are used in the community.

This part of the YOPP is still rather general. People are asked to think broadly about the way the community is dealing with important contributing factors. Since they are expressing their beliefs and opinions, the results are subjective in nature. The purpose of the YOPP, though, is to encourage people to think critically about what is happening in their community and to stimulate them to think about aspects of community realities in ways they might not have considered before. Importantly, the information about their

Figure 2. THE YOUTH OPPORTUNITY PLANNING PROCESS
Results of Part II – Questions "C" and "D"

Group: A southeastern community group Date: 8/24 – 28/81 N= 23

CONTRIBUTING FACTORS	No. of ✓	A. INDIVIDUAL/ SITUATIONAL		B. YOUTH/ ADULT		C. REMEDIATION/ PREVENTION		D. INDIVIDUALS/ CONDITIONS	
		Group Average	Range	Group Average	Range	Group Average	Range	Group Average	Range
1. Poor parenting and broken family ties. (224)	1	7.5	5-9	7.8	5-9	6.0	3-9	4.8	1-9
2. Schools fail to meet the needs of students. (163)	10	7.8	5-9	7.0	3-9	6.4	3-9	6.9	3-9
3. Negative peer pressure. (150)	0	3.6	1-8	2.3	1-5	5.3	1-9	3.3	1-8
4. Lack of economic, physiological and psychological stability. (138)	3	7.3	3-9	5.7	1-9	6.2	1-9	4.7	1-9
5. Lack of employment and vocational training and outdated child labor laws. (110) (Tie)	1	7.8	5-9	7.4	5-9	5.8	1-9	7.8	5-9
6. Easy access to drugs and alcohol. (110) (Tie)	7	4.2	1-9	4.6	1-8	5.8	1-9	6.1	1-9
7. Inadequacies of juvenile justice system. (95)	0	8.6	3-9	8.5	6-9	5.9	1-9	7.7	5-9
8. Attitudes of the community as a whole toward the juvenile delinquency problem. (89)	2	7.2	1-9	6.8	5-9	7.0	2-9	5.3	1-9
9. Lack of youth involvement in community planning. (82)	0	7.0	1-9	6.9	5-9	5.7	1-9	6.0	4-9
10. Inadequate recreational opportunities. (77)	6	7.8	2-9	7.2	5-9	5.9	1-9	7.4	5-9
CROSS FACTOR GROUP AVERAGES	1.3	6.9	–	6.4	–	6.0	–	6.0	–

community generated through this process is *their information.* They produce it, and it reflects their perceptions about their community. Even though it is based upon opinion it is probable that it is reasonably accurate. Part III of the YOPP provides for the gathering of more accurate information, so the opinions expressed in Part II can be refined and altered later.

The diversity of opinion that comes out as people respond to these questions becomes a new resource to the group. This can be demonstrated rather dramatically by forming a *people scale* in the workshop room. This is done simply by placing numbers from one to nine on an open wall of the room. After participants have completed one of the questions, they can go to the number on the wall that they used for a particular factor. This graphically displays the range of opinion, and while participants stand before the numbers they selected some useful discussion can occur through sharing reasons for their opinions. Various ways of looking at the factor are brought out, which underscores the value of different vantage points.

These kinds of insights begin to emerge in the first two or three hours of the Community Development Workshop as the participants complete structured workshop activities. The credibility of the data generated is quite high because group members are generating the data themselves. Respect for the data is important because it indicates respect for the participants and their perceptions of their community. Some of these perceptions may indeed be inaccurate on the part of some people in the group. The discussion of the factors can help to clarify a variety of matters related to them. When an entire group of knowledgeable people perceive the situation in much the same way, though, impressive evidence about existing conditions begins to take shape. Other workshop activities add to this evidence.

Probing the Results of Part II of the YOPP

The tabulated results of Part II of the YOPP can yield a significant amount of insight about the community, how it uses its resources and how strategies for human services in all four arenas of human service activity might be shaped and designed.

Some important observations can readily be gleaned from the data found in Figure 2. In relation to Question "A", the group believed that only two of the 10 most important contributing factors were within the control of the individual young person. The other eight factors were viewed as situational and beyond the control of the individual. The cross-factor group average for this factor was 6.9. This insight has immediate implications for the shaping of human service strategy.

Regarding the Youth Behavior/Adult Behavior Scale (Question "B") the participants believed that in relation to only one factor should the primary emphasis clearly be on changing youth behavior. One factor was near the mid-point (5) of the nine point scale, and the other eight showed a clear preference for emphasizing adult behavior change. The cross factor group average for that factor was 6.4. This, too, raises some critically important questions about the ways efforts to confront youth problems are currently designed.

In response to the Remediation/Prevention Scale (Question C), the group preferred an emphasis on prevention strategies in relation to all 10 factors, with a cross factor group average of 6.0. On the Individual Change/Condition Change Scale (Question D), views on three of the 10 factors showed a preference for an individual focus and on the other seven for a focus on changing conditions. The cross factor group average was 6.0.

By using the Arenas of Human Service Activity as a matrix (the horizontal line is the Purpose Continuum and reflects responses to Question C, while the vertical line is the Focus Continuum and reflects responses to Question D), it is possible to plot the group's responses as members think strategies should be designed (the preferred approach) and as they see resources currently being used (the perceived approach). These reflect their perceptions of Condition B and Condition A respectively. Figure 3 shows clearly that the preferred strategies fall within the prevention quadrants, mostly in Quadrant 1, while the current use of resources falls completely within Quadrant 4. The shaded areas demonstrate a significant discrepancy between what the group thinks would be a sound approach and what is current practice. *This pattern of response is the typical outcome of the use of the YOPP.*

What does this contrast indicate about the current patterns of human service design and the relevance of human service organizations to the realities of the community? The preference indicated by every group of people with which this process has been used is for a strong emphasis on prevention strategies that are focused on changing conditions that affect people. At the same time, the perceptions about current use of resources are that they are strongly reactive, remedial and focused upon individual change.

If, indeed, the factors which contribute to youth problems are predominantly situational in nature, beyond the control of individual young people and best approached through strategies focused upon changing adult behavior, it would seem that major reordering, reorganization and redesign of the youth service system is called for in most communities. Undertaking such a drastic change in emphasis borders upon a small revolution, and there are numerous vested interests that would be challenged by such a departure from what exists now. The experience of the Community Development Workshop, though, is that people usually see this challenge as an exciting one. They see it as a positive goal to work toward, and one that is based upon their own perceptions of their community.

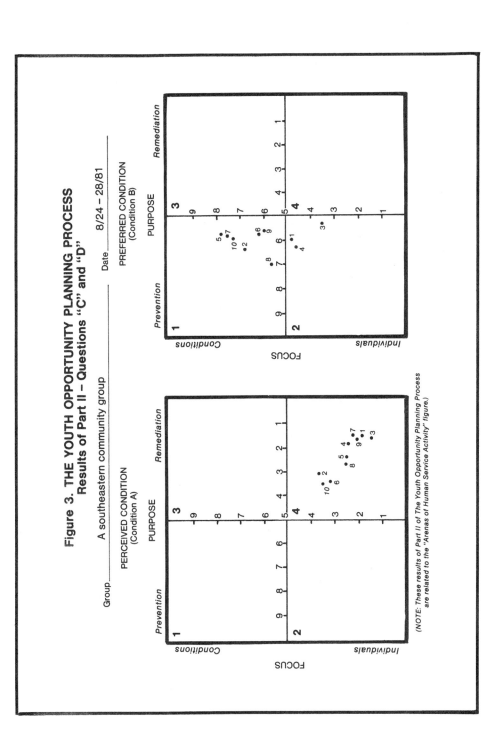

Figure 3. THE YOUTH OPPORTUNITY PLANNING PROCESS
Results of Part II – Questions "C" and "D"

Group _____ A southeastern community group _____ Date _____ 8/24 – 28/81

PERCEIVED CONDITION
(Condition A)

PREFERRED CONDITION
(Condition B)

(NOTE: These results of Part II of The Youth Opportunity Planning Process are related to the "Arenas of Human Service Activity" figure.)

The use of the YOPP in a number of communities and with a number of state level groups leads to the observation that *(1) human service systems and the specific organizations which make them up are not designed as people generally believe they should be, (2) service strategies are not as relevant to the realities of the community as they might be and (3) those responsible for shaping, leading, managing and working in human service systems lack some of the necessary concepts, tools, strategies and skills for redirecting the ways resources are used by the system.* An obvious aspect of this disturbing situation is that the strength of the Survival/Maintenance Mode and the prescriptive forces at work at the local, state and national levels serve to protect vested interests and perpetuate organizational and institutional patterns with which people are generally comfortable, though they are not as relevant to community needs as they might be.

Recognizing these conditions is only the beginning of the effort to discover the meaning of prevention. The YOPP can be expanded as its users are challenged to probe into their local situations. For example, another question that can be asked in relation to each factor is how many people the participants believe are affected by it. Does the factor affect virtually all people, a significant majority, about half, a significant minority, or very few? Perceptions such as these can add to the assessment of existing conditions and later become useful for action planning purposes.

COMMON CONDITIONS AFFECTING PEOPLE IN MOST COMMUNITIES

An important frontier in American society is the need to help, encourage and assure that community institutions and organizations become more responsible and responsive to the needs of people. This is an essential part of the process of relating resources to needs, and it is an essential aspect of prevention as it is being proposed. Indeed, *it is a community responsibility to see that institutions are viable and relevant.* There is too much evidence that when public institutions are not held accountable they tend to become distant, unresponsive, irrelevant and wasteful of community resources. Beyond that, they can even contribute negatively to the lives of people.

Another experiential training strategy used in the Community Development Workshop calls attention to three kinds of conditions which daily affect the lives of numerous people. These conditions are reflected in the quality of opportunities available to people and are related to important decisions that are made routinely. Perhaps because they are both routine and pervasive, these conditions go unquestioned year after year in most communities.

Again, this training activity has been used to focus upon youth development, but it can be directed toward other groups or concerns as well. The first condition deals with youth participation, the second with decisions about resources and the third with organizational design. The activity is called

"Common Conditions Affecting Young People in Most Communities." It is designed to raise for workshop participants practical and fundamental questions which become an important part of viewing the community from a prevention perspective.

First, there are philosophical questions about the nature of institutions in a democratic society. How well do organizations foster democratic principles? Do the various human service organizations of the community, both public and private, really "belong to the people" or do they belong to an isolated few who happen to control them at a given point in time?

Second, how relevant are various institutions and their constituent organizations to the needs of people? What kind of effort is made to understand those needs and to increase and maintain a high level of relevance to them?

Third, what kinds of knowledge and skill do those in key leadership positions have for fostering democratic processes to improve opportunities for people in the community? How are leaders held accountable for developing and using those skills effectively?

Fourth, do the prevailing practices in the community promote among its residents a sense of ownership of community organizations and their operation? Too often there is a cynical attitude about "unchanging and unchangeable bureaucracy," and people frequently see community apathy as an insurmountable obstacle in the way of bringing about positive community change.

This workshop activity has been designed as a strategy for helping a group of people develop specific ways to bring about change in institutional patterns. The first step in that direction is to describe the condition in clear and specific terms (Condition A) so that planned action can then follow.

Condition I – Youth Participation

How do youth serving organizations relate to the young people for whom they provide opportunities? Do they view young people simply as the recipients of their services, or do they give young people an opportunity to become actively involved in important aspects of their operations? There may be many attitudes in the community about how much participation on the part of young people is appropriate and desirable, and those attitudes can have a profound effect on the organization. The first part of this activity provides the participants in the Community Development Workshop an opportunity to examine the predominant patterns of organizational life as they relate to the following question:

> In the planning, operation and evaluation of opportunities that exist
> for the well-being of young people, are young people systematically
> excluded, or is their participation encouraged and welcomed?

Participants are asked to indicate their perceptions about this question as they consider the wide range of youth-serving organizations in their community. This is done on the scale below.

1	2	3	4	5	6	7	8	9	10

Encouraged and   Systematically
welcomed   excluded

As with the YOPP process, the opinions and perceptions of the people involved can be numerically tabulated. This question has consistently resulted in a response of between 7.0 and 8.5 on the scale. This indicates a belief that the tendency toward systematic exclusion of young people from participation in significant aspects of youth-focused organizations is quite strong.

Next the participants are asked to develop a list of youth-focused organizations in their community that have found ways to encourage and welcome youth participation in their planning, operation and evaluation processes. As an organization is identified, the person naming it is asked to describe what methods that organization has developed to promote youth involvement. This not only emphasizes the positive, but it becomes instructive for members of organizations which have no such methods. It also means that each organization that is added to the list must stand the scrutiny of the group. Experience has shown that, even in larger communities, this list tends to be quite short.

The next task for the participants is to develop a list of reasons why, if a pattern of exclusion exists in the community and its organizations, that pattern is there. This activity usually helps to identify a number of negative qualities, such as fear on the part of the adults who control the organizations, lack of skill and experience among adults to foster youth participation, lack of skill and experience among young people to participate "responsibly," long standing patterns of youth exclusion, and the beliefs that "young people lack the wisdom to make responsible decisions" and "adults know what is best for young people."

Frequently, many of the adults involved in this discussion begin to see that, although a pattern of youth exclusion prevails, such does not need to be the case. Once the pattern is recognized, tangible and specific steps can be taken to change it. When young people are responsibly participating in this discussion with adults, the fact of their systematic exclusion from meaningful participation in the very organizations which exist to address their needs becomes even more poignant.

The participants next are asked to develop a list of general ideas that might be pursued to change this condition to one in which *young people are systematically included in the planning, operation and evaluation of opportunities that exist for their well-being.* This kind of thinking can stimulate group members to commit themselves to doing something about such a condition in their community. That they are in fact doing something about it by participating in the workshop, young people and adults together, demonstrates its value. Transferring this experience to the community at many levels and in many places becomes part of the action planning focus of the workshop.

Condition II – Decisions about Resources

What kinds of information inform the decisions of those in policy-making positions as they allocate the resources at their disposal for youth opportunities? Insight into the real nature of these decision processes can tell much about the community and help to clarify the conditions under which an emphasis on prevention must be pursued. The community simulation activity which focuses on the shaping of prevention policy described in Chapter III also deals with this important area of community life.

This consideration is introduced to participants by asking them to respond to the following question:

Are decisions about resources for young people based upon a systematic assessment of the needs, informed choices and desires of young people, or are they the result of other factors (such as the perceptions, subjective conclusions and biases of adult decision makers, expectations placed upon them by other adults, traditions in decision patterns and prescriptive forces shaped by adults)?

Again, participants are asked to express their perceptions about this question as it relates to the range of youth-serving organizations in their community by using this scale.

1	2	3	4	5	6	7	8	9	10

Based upon a systematic assessment

Based upon the biases, etc. of adults

Experience with this question has consistently yielded responses that fall between 7.5 and 9.0 on the scale. This indicates a strong perception that a systematic assessment of the needs, informed choices and desires of young people is seldom used in decision making.

The next step is for participants to identify the individuals and decision groups in the community who exercise the most influence on decisions about the allocation of resources for young people. The nature of the decisions made or influenced by these persons or groups can also be clarified.

After this the group is asked to discuss what kinds of information, beliefs or values those decision makers appear to use as a basis for their decisions, as well as the sources of their information for decision making. This can become the focus of some informal inquiry similar to that suggested in the section entitled "Does Your Community Have a Well-defined Prevention Policy?" in Chapter III. A sampling of decision makers might be interviewed to develop more specific awareness of how decisions actually are made.

An objective assessment of the ways resource allocation decisions are made can lead to some action strategies by community people that can have a profound effect on institutions. This can become an important part of a community prevention strategy. If the existing patterns effectively help to facilitate the allocation of resources to needs, then no change may be seen as desirable. On the other hand, if there is little rationale in the current pattern, then an action strategy to promote a more responsible approach may be needed. The results of this kind of discussion have consistently pointed toward the latter.

Condition III – Organizational Design

A related matter, and one that was focused upon in Chapter III, has to do with the forces which shape organizational design. The processes through which local organizations determine how they will use their resources is especially important to prevention for several reasons. It is more likely that the proactive, developmentally shaped strategies of prevention will result from the involvement of local people addressing local conditions than from programs shaped by the prescriptive forces that reside outside the local community. This proposition needs to be tested against the realities of the community. Second, since rather highly prescribed organizations tend to make up the major portion of human service resources in the community, it is useful to encourage people to consider what this reality means for the building of prevention capability. Third, it is not uncommon for the leadership and many of the participants in a local prevention initiative to come from highly prescribed organizations. Focusing upon how those organizations and their staffs can participate creatively and with flexibility in a collaborative prevention effort becomes an important consideration.

The question used to deal with organizational design is as follows:

How are local youth-serving organizations shaped? Are they shaped more by local people, based upon their perceptions of local needs and conditions, or do they tend to be shaped more by forces from outside the community?

1	2	3	4	5	6	7	8	9	10
Shaped by local people					Shaped by outside forces				

Workshop participants tend to have more difficulty generalizing about this question than the others because of the somewhat subtle nature of the various forces that act upon local organizations. The usual average response falls between 6.5 and 8.0, suggesting that people perceive a high degree of outside prescriptive influence on organizational design within their communities.

The identification of organizations which are shaped through an on-going developmental process and discussion of how that process takes place is useful for focusing on the dynamics of organizational design. Most communities have relatively few such organizations. Other, more prescribed organizations which have developed a high level of responsiveness to local conditions can also be identified. Discussion of the factors which make this possible can provide an understanding of how this flexibility can be encouraged. Beyond this, the identification of those factors which tend to inhibit organizations from being more responsive to local needs and conditions provides valuable information for action planning.

Effective prevention strategies will probably involve working with and through the highly prescribed organizations of the community as well as with other resources which can more easily be engaged. As key people from these organizations become involved in creative, developmental prevention efforts there is a possibility that some influence upon certain aspects of organizational design, such as refocusing job descriptions and reallocating staff time, will take place. Placing more emphasis on prevention at the policy and management levels is a longer term goal to work toward.

USING A PREVENTION PERSPECTIVE

The Community Development Workshop is a training strategy that encourages people to look at their community from a prevention perspective and then to develop action plans based upon that perspective which pursue specific goals in their community. Some of the workshop activities which have been designed to provide an experiential approach to this have been described. These include "Organizational Lifestyles and Prevention," "Developing a Community Youth Policy," "The Youth Opportunity Planning Process (Parts I and II)," and "Common Conditions Affecting Young People in Most Communities." A number of other ideas, frameworks and models have been described which also encourage people to think about prevention and its importance for their community. These ideas and training activities have been useful in encouraging individuals to give prevention more consideration and in equipping groups of people for the task of organizing themselves to provide technical assistance to others in their states and local communities in the interest of prevention.

The essential purpose of training is to change the behavior of the trainees. The Community Development Workshop is designed to change the behavior of people in policy making, management and service delivery positions, as well as other potential resource people who might become involved in carrying out an assertive prevention program. Many people who have participated in Community Development Workshops, whether in a local setting or as part of a statewide prevention initiative, have found that these ideas and training experiences have equipped them with new concepts, strategies, tools and skills for the task of promoting interest and involvement in prevention.

The response to this training experience has indicated that many of the participants have gained a new sense of direction for using a prevention perspective. Comments from some participants are as follows:

"Renews my faith... An exciting concept... Gives me renewed spirit and a new direction... Good for me and hopefully for those I serve."

"I've been involved in prevention efforts for some time but have never actually experienced the method by which those prevention concepts are taught and made available to communities. By participating I was able to get a handle on the more concrete, experiential aspects of prevention."

(Comments of a young person) "The strengths of the workshop for me were the adults' willingness to listen to me, I was able to contribute more to the group tasks and discussions than I thought I would, and my growth through the workshop activities, tasks and discussions. I would like to see more of this type of workshop done. It gets to the root of some or most of the community's problems and it is an incentive to get something going in the community. It broadens horizons and makes people aware."

"The workshop was very helpful in introducing new ways to deal with bringing about change through prevention concepts. These refreshing approaches will help stimulate me to try to bring about change in my community."

"The youth involvement, the well prepared flow of activities, the materials and the level of commitment among the people who attended were strong features of the workshop. This workshop was really significant to me. I am committed to youth involvement, proactive change (individual and systems), and community education. I am now much better prepared."

While participant comments such as these do not reflect any actual behavior change, they do indicate clearly that their perceptions at the end of the workshop experience were in keeping with the purpose of the workshop.

The kind of prevention perspective proposed in this book encourages a critical look at conditions in the community and the ways the organized resources are relating to those conditions. Strong emphasis has been placed on organizational and institutional change because it is apparent that even a modest change in organizational emphasis can frequently have significant influence on conditions that are causing the symptoms people are interested in preventing. The concepts and skills required for organizational change are the same ones required for promoting change in other community conditions. The supportive experience of exploring community change with others who occupy different positions and have different viewpoints of the community can be the stimulus that helps to initiate a new action program in a community.

One of the most important qualities of a prevention perspective, when it is fostered through a practical training experience, is that it gives hope. Because of the tendency of many organizations to become caught in "the activity trap" and expend their resources in reactive services, numerous human service professionals are questioning the value of much of what they do. A prevention perspective raises fundamental questions about what can best be done to gain the most positive results in relation to specific community problems and aspirations. Another common condition with many organizations is related to their management capability, and a prevention perspective encourages a more purposeful approach to assessing current conditions, shaping achievable goals and designing action plans to attain them. This requires sound management of resources. These two areas of organizational experience are the source of considerable frustration among professionals and community citizens alike. A prevention perspective can help to raise provocative questions and point toward some valuable new directions for human service organizations and other community oriented groups.

OCCASIONS FOR ACTION

Viewing the community from a prevention perspective provides a number of valuable starting points for undertaking an assertive prevention initiative. The YOPP identifies some general areas of community life toward which prevention action programs can be addressed. A variety of organizational and institutional conditions have been suggested which invite programs of planned change at the policy, management and service levels. The problem for those interested in prevention becomes one of deciding with which of all of the options to start.

Still another way of viewing the community from a prevention perspective is to select from the wide variety of common, everyday occurrences that any community experiences and use an event as a starting point for shaping a prevention action plan. If this is seen as a negative event, such as some of those described below, it may appear that this would be a reactive, Quadrant 3 type of response. It is possible, though, to use such an event to serve as the starting point of a Quadrant 1 action plan if those involved persist through a response to the immediate situation. To prepare the participants in a Community Development Workshop for such an undertaking, a training activity has been designed which is called "Occasions for Action."

This activity addresses several matters of practical importance to people who are interested in getting specific results from their energy and resources. It demonstrates (1) how time is a valuable resource that is often wasted; (2) the value of a framework for being task oriented, productive and efficient; (3) the benefits of clearly stated policy guidelines for making decisions; and (4) the idea that common, everyday events can become the stimulus for positive, assertive initiatives to create new conditions that promote the well-being of people. This activity has been designed as the transitional experience to help the participants in the Community Development Work-shop shift from a consideration of viewing the community from a prevention perspective to action planning, so it is fitting to include it here as a step into the next chapter on Planning for Action.

A restricted time frame is used for this highly structured activity. The participants are divided into small work groups and given a description of a rather common situation that might occur in their community. They are also given some simple policy directives and a simple decision-making framework which consists of four questions. The groups are given 12 minutes in which to complete their task.

The simple policy directives are (1) to develop a work plan that uses existing resources and does not require new funding, (2) to include young people as active participants in the development of an action plan, and (3) to place an emphasis on using the people resources of the community.

Following are examples of common situations that can be used as a focus for this activity:

Situation #1

Over the summer months groups of teenagers began congregating outside a quick-serve hamburger place in a shopping center in the early evening. This happened spontaneously, and the spot soon became "the place to go." As the numbers of youths grew, complaints from the merchants began to increase and police began patrolling the shopping center.

A formal complaint to the city council led one night to an encounter between police and the young people. Police asked the group, about 300 young people in all, to leave and not to use the parking lot as a gathering place any more.

The next night the young people returned and some heated verbal exchanges took place between them and the police.

A newspaper reporter investigating the situation interviewed some of the young people, who said they had no other place to get together and found the shopping center parking lot to their liking. It was easy to get to, and food was available. No place else in the city had those features.

The police who were interviewed said complaints from merchants required that they disperse the young people.

Situation #2

There has been a sudden interest in drag racing among teenagers on a particular stretch of road on the north side of the city. Two days ago an accident occurred which resulted in some damaged property, a totaled car, and slight injuries to two of the young people.

The Sheriff's Department has put up some roadblocks to control this activity and is patrolling the road frequently.

Situation #3

A large number of young people plan a marathon walk to raise funds for developing and improving playground facilities in a low income section of the city. As a result, they raise $720 which they turn over to the City Recreation Department.

The newspaper provides good coverage of the walk and commends the young people who organized it as well as those who participate. The story points out that this kind of positive action is unusual and it would be desirable to have more of it.

Situation #4

A particular junior high school has developed a reputation for being a trouble spot. A number of instances of vandalism have been reported, the absentee and dropout rates at the school are well above the district average, and there is an observable increase in the use of drugs and alcohol among the students. Concern is growing that even younger children are being influenced in these matters.

The police, juvenile court and mental health center all indicate that a disproportionate amount of their activity occurs in the general vicinity of this school.

The principal believes strongly that "lack of parental support" is the basis of the difficulties at the school. A number of parents have expressed strong concern about the lack of safety for them and their children in the neighborhoods of the area. The young people, when asked, state that a lack of leisure time opportunities, meaningless schools, no jobs, and hassles from the police are the real problems.

There is a general feeling in the area that it is the forgotten, by-passed part of the city. People believe that no one cares, so nothing is done. The gestures of previous years to "rehabilitate" the area were of little avail.

The discussion guide for considering each of the situations is as follows:

1. Using this situation (Condition A) as a starting point, describe some conditions that would be appropriate goals to work toward (Condition B).
2. List several kinds of resource people who could be useful for developing an action plan.
3. To make positive use of this situation, what would be a useful first step? Why?
4. What do you see as the potential for a cooperative, coordinated community effort in this situation and how might this be encouraged?

After each work group has reported on its discussion, some useful observations about what happened are made. People who have participated in this activity have consistently pointed out that the short time factor, the framework for discussion and the policy guidelines all contribute to being task-oriented and productive. The energy level in the groups is always quite high, there is total participation among all the group members, and there is a high level of satisfaction among the group members with the outcomes of their discussion. There is never any extraneous discussion or monopolizing of the group by individual members. Group members are also pleasantly surprised with how much they cover in a very short period of time. In short, the relationship between structure, clear policy and productivity becomes rather clear. It is usually observed that these qualities are seldom present in the many meetings that group members continually find themselves in.

The concept of using common everyday events in the community as "occasions for action" can help a small group of people concerned about prevention to become aware of useful starting points. This activity also brings together ideas about assertive approaches that have been presented in the workshop: focusing on conditions, engaging key allies for positive change and using a developmental process for creating conditions that promote the well-being of people. The benefits of having policy that equips people and organizations with the direction and structure they need to make things happen in a positive manner is demonstrated.

Encouraging and preparing people for viewing the community from a prevention perspective requires, for some people, new ways of thinking about community change, the use of available resources and the possibilities of improving community conditions that affect people in important ways. If this can happen with even a small group of people who become committed to the task of prevention it is possible to achieve some significant results.

Viewing the community from a prevention perspective can open up a wide range of possibilities for positive community action that can benefit numbers of people. There are many situations which almost automatically are "programmed" for a remedial response that focuses on individuals. If seen as "occasions for action" in a preventive sense, these situations might be approached in a variety of ways that prove to be creative and beneficial.

□

chapter 5
Planning
For Action

To make prevention a practical process of planned change which creates new conditions that promote the well-being of people requires a carefully designed combination of information, skills and resources. The change process involves three steps: knowing what it is one wishes to change (Condition A), deciding what new condition one wishes to exist (Condition B), and developing and implementing a set of strategies to get from A to B.

At each of these steps one must deal realistically and assertively with organizational and institutional patterns. This requires a set of tools capable of achieving the desired results. It also requires constant awareness that our democratic society places special importance on the word *participation*. We value the concept of each person's having a part in shaping the community within which he or she lives.

A community development approach to prevention, then, sees the "people resources" of the community as key components in the process. The service options of prevention that have been identified must be mobilized and coordinated in practical and specific ways if they are to become useful to people. The Community Development Workshop offers one way to equip people for this task. Some other approach to placing the necessary tools in the hands of people who can use them is possible but the basic task of those who promote prevention remains the same.

At this point the workability of the approach to prevention receives its hardest tests. This chapter focuses upon some action tools that can be used and suggests ways that the key allies for prevention can plot their course and build and maintain community support.

FIRST STEPS TOWARDS PLANNED CHANGE

The tools to be presented in this chapter are built upon the essential ingredients of the change process that were introduced in Chapter II. Describing Condition A and Condition B at first may appear to be quite simple, but it is in fact a very difficult task. This is probably because we are oriented so strongly toward symptoms and activities. We seldom think through the nature of existing conditions we would like to change and clearly describe the conditions we would like to achieve.

A simple worksheet can be helpful. It is called the "Condition A/Condition B/Indicator Worksheet." The first step is to select a specific condition that needs changing and to describe it in clear and specific terms in several sentences. The second step is to describe in equally clear and specific terms a desirable and achievable condition that could replace the first condition. A simple, limited situation is suggested for practicing these steps.

This worksheet introduces another dimension: the task of developing a set of tangible indicators that can be used to measure or monitor progress from Condition A to Condition B. These indicators should be specific and completely practical. They might relate to information that is currently being collected or they might point toward new information that would be useful. If it proves difficult to think of specific indicators, it may be because the Condition A and Condition B statements are not specific enough, in which case they should be reviewed, and possibly revised.

To use a relatively simple example, a school principal is concerned about vandalism in the school. The concern results from such matters as the number of broken windows which have needed replacement over the past year. There may be other symptoms that can also be described in clear terms. A key question for exploring Condition A and developing some useful descriptive statements is "What are the conditions under which these symptoms occur?" Some open and honest discussion among key people at the school can help to shape these statements. This group would probably include students, teachers and administrators. If the facts about the symptoms show, for example, that 90 windows were repaired last year compared with 38 during the previous year, the Condition A statements should describe the conditions under which this symptom occurred. The Condition B statements then should describe the circumstances under which these symptoms are unlikely or less likely to occur. The number of broken windows becomes a useful indicator by which progress can be gauged. Obviously, the clarity of the relationship between the current condition, the indicator and the desired outcome is a key to the success of the change process to be introduced.

Undertaking these first planning steps before getting into the kinds of activities that will move you from where you are to where you want to be serves several useful purposes. It provides a basis for gauging your progress, a matter to be explored in some detail in the next chapter. It protects the planning group from jumping into the activity trap or from trying to fit someone else's "solutions" to the situation that is of concern. It also helps a group of people to discover the power of focusing on conditions without placing blame on individuals. In short, it provides the basis for building some realistic steps toward positive change.

As students, teachers and administrators consider their school, they might determine, for example, that students do not feel they have a part in making the decisions which shape their school, are lacking in "school spirit" and feel alienated from the school. These feelings make up a Condition A. If it then is decided that a desirable outcome is substantial ownership among students of shaping and determining the nature of their school (a Condition B), some useful indicators of progress may relate to the frequency of opportunities students have for interacting with policy makers, administrators and teachers in changing specific aspects of the school community. Monitoring of the specific impacts of strategies agreed upon on various aspects of the school can be helpful. Thoughtfully relating these opportunities to the indicators of vandalism can help to determine if there is a relationship between student involvement in shaping the school and the amount of symptomatic behavior directed negatively toward the school.

An important fork in the planning road occurs here, one branch of which leads to Quadrant 3 (Community Problem Solving) and the other to Quadrant 1 (Community Development). There is a strong tendency on the part of administrators and other people who have a controlling influence on organizations and institutions to think in terms of "stopping the symptom from happening." In this example, to follow this tendency would be to determine that the desirable outcome, or Condition B, is to achieve a normal number of broken windows, say 25 per year. If reducing window breakage is seen as the goal rather than an indicator of a more positive condition, then the road toward Quadrant 3 has been taken. This is essentially a remedial way of thinking and the action strategy can appropriately be called "deterrence," or stopping something from happening.

On the other hand, if one uses the number of broken windows as one of several positive indicators that are related to the achievement of the desired outcome, a qualitatively different strategy to achieve the outcome can be pursued. Relating this approach to planning to the positive mission of the school as an educational institution requires a different mindset from the more remedial, reactive mindset of problem solving. To take the more positive route and to use the broken windows as an "occasion for action" which leads to the positive potential of Quadrant 1 becomes a crucial choice for those in leadership positions. Indeed, it is a clear choice which has immediate, practical implications for numbers of people. In this example, the outcome of this choice can affect large numbers of students, teachers and administrators in tangible, measurable ways. Obviously, using a strategy which simply addresses a reduction in the number of broken windows will probably be quite different from a strategy which increases student and teacher involvement in shaping a positive learning environment that is characterized by a high degree of student ownership and pride in "their school."

Three planning models that build on these ideas are introduced in this chapter. If used well, systematic planning and action models can become powerful tools for achieving desired results. Numerous change models have been devised for various purposes. In his book, *Visualizing Change: Model Building and the Change Process,*[6] Gordon Lippitt presents a variety of change models focused upon human resource development and individual, group and organizational change. He also discusses skills in developing change models. The reader is encouraged to become familiar with a number of change models and to use those best suited for a particular purpose.

The three specific tools for planning and action presented in this chapter can be introduced easily to a group of people. They are simple in concept, direct in approach and provide a basis for assessing progress. While they are similar in some respects, each has qualities that lend it to special use. They can be used together in sequence, or they can be used separately, as will become clear after they have been described and illustrated.

The elements of the change process are further illustrated in Figure 4. Each of the models presented, it should be noted, is a generic process model. That is to say any of them can be used in relation to change in any of the four arenas of human service activity, or to any kind of change process for that matter.

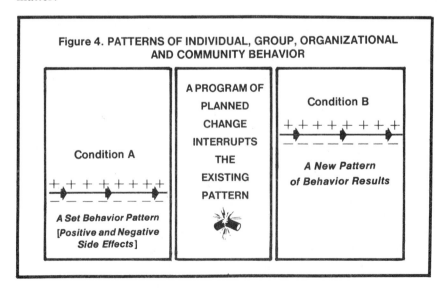

Figure 4. PATTERNS OF INDIVIDUAL, GROUP, ORGANIZATIONAL
AND COMMUNITY BEHAVIOR

Condition A

A Set Behavior Pattern
[Positive and Negative
Side Effects]

A PROGRAM OF
PLANNED
CHANGE
INTERRUPTS
THE
EXISTING
PATTERN

Condition B

A New Pattern
of Behavior Results

THE PREVENTION FORMULA

The Prevention Formula[7] is a useful tool for efficiently gaining a sense of direction and examining some of the dynamics of the change to be sought. It uses mathematical symbols to focus upon a positive community process of planned change. In the formula:

$$\frac{A}{bc(RP)} \longrightarrow B$$

"A" represents *conditions as they are* (the problem, need, area of concern);

"B" represents the *desired result* (the goal);

"bc" represents the *behavior change* that will be required to allow substantial change from A to B;

"R" represents the *resources* (human, physical, financial) needed to support the change from A to B;

"P" represents the *participation of those key controlling people who have the capability of exercising influence over Condition A*;

$\longrightarrow$ represents the resulting strategy that leads to Condition B.

Several observations can be made about the formula and its symbolism. The action in the formula is provided by the denominator, $bc(RP)$. It is the denominator that acts upon Condition A. The symbol for "yields" (the arrow) is used instead of an "equals" sign because Condition B is not just a reduction of Condition A. That is to say, the interaction between Condition A and the forces that will be working to change it, $bc(RP)$, are dynamic and the nature of Condition B need not be just a rearrangement or lessening of Condition A. In fact, as a description of an effective prevention process, Condition B will be an enriched, more dynamic and more desirable condition than Condition A.

In $bc(RP)$, the three elements involved interact with each other with a multiplier effect. As R and P become involved, the process of behavior change has already begun. As the amount of behavior change increases, the interaction between R and P and their relationships to both A and B become more significant. On the other hand, if bc, R or P is seen as having a value of zero, the whole denominator would equal zero, and no change would occur in Condition A. Obviously, then, the goal, or B, would not be achieved. This suggests that the forces represented by $bc(RP)$ will need to be of such nature that they are able to have a significant impact on A. It is important to note, too, that if people who can exercise some control over A (P) become a part of R, which would make them key allies, those persons become part of the solution. Otherwise they remain a part of the problem (Condition A).

The Prevention Formula can be put to work in practical and specific ways. The following steps combine to make a brief Prevention Formula Worksheet. These steps can be used to develop a work plan. Working together, several people who have a perspective on the matter being dealt with can combine their insights efficiently and productively.

THE PREVENTION FORMULA WORKSHEET

Step I
Briefly describe with a series of simple statements the essential aspects of Condition A. (The current situation)

Step II
Briefly describe with a series of simple statements the essential aspects of Condition B. (The desired result)

Step III
List those specific people (P) who are in a position to exercise some control over Condition A. (Place a check mark by those you think might become positively involved in pursuing Condition B as key allies.)

Step IV
Briefly describe with a series of simple statements the kinds of behavior change (bc) that will enable a change from Condition A to Condition B.

Step V
Briefly describe the human, physical and financial resources (R) needed to enable a change from Condition A to Condition B.

It is useful in completing step V to emphasize methods that use the existing human, physical and financial resources of the community and deemphasize the need for new financial resources.

The information generated through these five steps can be refined into a more specific work plan through the use of the next action model if that is needed. Just doing this much, though, can give a group of key allies a specific direction toward which their energies can be employed. The Prevention Formula is useful for "roughing out" a plan. It is efficient and encourages the use of simple descriptive statements. Frequently people make the task of planned change much more complex and difficult than it needs to be. Even a complicated situation can be described with a series of simple statements. Again, the more clearly the Condition A is described, the easier it will be to describe Condition B.

An experience with a Native American group in northern Arizona serves as a clear illustration of the use of the Prevention Formula. The occasion was an all day training session with the Community Youth Council. A dozen high school students were invited to participate in the session, along with the adult members of the council.

While discussing the formula, the group was asked to suggest an example of a situation they would like to change. The young people suggested a focus on the lunches in the high school cafeteria. (The students had just returned from lunch.) First, they were asked to describe the condition of the lunches they would like to change (Condition A). They rather quickly made these statements, which were written as stated before the group.

"The lunches are not hot when they are served."
"The lunches have little variety from day to day."
"The lunches have little nutritional value."
"The servings we get do not fit our appetites."
"The lunches usually are not attractive."
"The food often smells bad."
"The lunches frequently taste bad."

When they were satisfied that these statements adequately described the situation as they saw it, they were asked what result they would like to have (Condition B). They studied the statements before them and immediately saw that by changing a word here and there they could describe the desired condition, as follows:

"We would like the food to be hot when it is served."
"We would like more variety in the food."
"We want food with more nutritional value."
"We would like appropriate-sized servings."
"We would like attractive food."
"We want the food to smell good."
"We want the food to taste good."

They were then asked to list the people they thought could exercise some control over Condition A. They quickly prepared a list which included the superintendent of schools, the high school principal, the director of the food service, the people who purchase the food, those who prepare the food and those who serve the food.

After a brief discussion of the kinds of behavior change that would be needed by each of these people to achieve Condition B, one of the adults in the group, who was a school administrator, said this change could probably be affected without any additional personnel, equipment or money.

The young people were asked how they would know if Condition B has been achieved. They suggested they could set up a student advisory group to monitor the food from week to week and to hear the opinions of the students.

This group could pass their observations along to the proper school staff people. They believed that, given the clarity of the goals, they would be able to tell how well the plan was working. This discussion took no longer than 20 minutes.

While this is a rather simple situation, it is instructive in that it illustrates how the Prevention Formula helped to focus the discussion very efficiently, the statements were descriptive and to the point, and the group felt purposive and satisfied that they had analyzed the situation appropriately. It illustrates, too, that if the descriptive statements get right to the heart of the matter, there is no need for lengthy, rambling discussion. *Being task oriented, efficient and productive in action planning will have its rewards!*

The following three case examples show how the Prevention Formula can be applied to a variety of practical situations.

Case Number 1 – Central Junior High School

Central Junior High School has for several years been beset with a number of problems. Evidence of this has included numerous instances of vandalism to the building, increasingly high absentee rates, frequent referrals of students to the principal's office for disciplinary action, an overall decrease in student achievement, and an increase in teacher requests to be transferred to other "more rewarding" educational environments. The pressures on the faculty and administration to find more effective ways to deal with these symptomatic realities and the apparent failure of their recent attempts to "keep the lid on" led them to look in new directions for effective solutions.

The principal and a faculty committee organized an effort to analyze the situation as a first step toward designing a solution. After one meeting, they decided they needed the participation of students. They invited six students to work with them, including some of the "worst trouble makers" they could identify. The students were skeptical at first, but, during the first meeting of this larger group, they began to get involved in the discussion of "their school." After three meetings, students and staff were satisfied they had developed an adequate understanding of the Condition A of Central Junior High School. They decided that during the next meeting they would focus upon Condition B, *what they wanted their school to be like.*

As a part of describing Condition A, the members of the committee talked with a large number of students, teachers, parents and school administrative staff. They began to get a good idea of peoples' attitudes, perspectives and degrees of willingness to become a part of whatever steps they might develop to change the situation. To the surprise of the adults on the committee, the students, even the "troublemakers," showed themselves to be mature participants in the whole effort. To the surprise of the students, the adults proved to be willing to listen, genuinely concerned about the students' educations, and interested in much more than "just their next paycheck."

As they began to determine what they wanted Condition B to be, they realized that they were not only resources for change (R), but that they were also people who could exercise some control over Condition A (P). They developed a list of others who controlled Condition A that included faculty members, students and key administrative staff. They also discussed the kinds of additional resource people (R) who could help.

It was something of a discovery that after only three weeks they began to notice some behavior change (bc) among themselves because of the new relationships that began to result from their conversations. They realized that by planning this process more specifically and consciously, they could foster more extensive behavior change more rapidly. This, in turn, would expand the participation of key controllers (P) and the whole experience became more attractive to new resources (R).

After six months, the committee was able to see that the specific concerns that were a part of Condition A had begun to change significantly. Vandalism within the school almost disappeared. Teachers were learning to handle "behavior problems" more ably in the classroom, and referrals to the principal's office decreased noticeably. There was also a slight decrease in the absentee rates during the fifth and sixth months. There was a general feeling, too, that the overall atmosphere in the school was less tense, more friendly and conducive to the educational purposes of the school.

Because of this desirable progress in moving toward Condition B, the committee decided that this program of planned change would need to receive continuing emphasis for an indefinite period of time. They realized that not only was it a source of real personal satisfaction for them and many others but that the new skills adults and students were developing for exercising responsible control over their school were, in fact, an important part of their learning. They were creating a new set of conditions that promoted the well-being of all persons involved. Thus, they discovered the meaning of the Prevention Formula.

Case Number 2 – The Smith Family

The Smith family consists of Mr. and Mrs. Smith and their four children, ages eight through 17. Throughout the 19 years of their marriage Mr. and Mrs. Smith have experienced periods of restrained animosity. They have tended to bicker frequently, and the relationships among their children have become intense sibling rivalries. The oldest child has become quite uncommunicative with his parents, and as the periods of silence between them have become more prolonged, Mr. and Mrs. Smith have become increasingly suspicious about how he spends his time when he is away from home. As Mr. and Mrs. Smith ponder the present and future of their family life it seems to point to increasing disintegration, a prospect that pleases them not at all. The fact that they know some of their close friends' experiences to be variations of this same theme gives them little consolation.

As Mrs. Smith was telling their youngest child "goodnight" one night, after a particularly uncomfortable evening of tension, the eight-year-old said she wished they could be happier at home. Mr. and Mrs. Smith discussed this later that night, and they promised each other they would do everything they could to improve their lives together.

After several weeks of uncertainty and not knowing where to turn, they heard about a parent education course that was to be offered, beginning the next week. They enrolled, along with eight other couples. Before the first class was over they began to sense that this might be just what they needed. The instructor was positive in his approach, and as he encouraged the class participants to think about the patterns of their family life and presented them with some practical concepts for understanding them, they relaxed and became more involved in the class.

The course included numerous activities that focused upon common experiences between parents and their children. Skills in listening and communicating were practiced, and clearcut steps for problem solving were learned, including the Prevention Formula. The class members were encouraged to use these skills at home and to discuss them openly with their children. Mr. and Mrs. Smith began to realize their deeply ingrained patterns of relating and their oft repeated behaviors were being challenged and were, in fact, changing.

The conditions of their family life became clearer to them as they proceeded through the course. They engaged their children in discussing what they thought had been happening (Condition A) and what they would like their relationships and family atmosphere to become (Condition B). Mr. and Mrs. Smith used the new skills they were learning as they talked with their children. A sense of what they wanted for themselves became clearer. The behavior changes (bc) that they discussed and which had begun to take place became apparent to all members of the family. The resources (R) represented by the parent training course helped them see that they could exercise more control over their own situation and become participants (P) in an exciting and satisfying venture at home.

After the eight-week course was over, Mr. and Mrs. Smith realized something significant was happening for all of them. Their oldest son became increasingly willing to interact with them as they used their new listening skills, and his periods away from home diminished.

An additional experience in a marriage enrichment group sponsored by a nearby church assisted Mr. and Mrs. Smith in strengthening the new directions they were shaping for themselves. After several months they had a deep awareness that they had indeed created new conditions which were promoting the well-being of all members of the family. They had discovered the use of the Prevention Formula.

Case Number 3 – The Brasstown Community

The Brasstown Community is a neighborhood located just outside the perimeter of the central city in a large urban area. Brasstown has been stable for many years but is now experiencing some new forces for change. Some new housing projects have been built and many new residents are moving in. This has had significant impact on the schools, the limited recreation resources and transportation. The rapid changes are having an unsettling effect on old and new residents alike.

Because of the obvious potentially negative consequences of this transition, several people got together for informal discussion of the situation. The group included a local minister, the principal of one of the schools, two businessmen and a couple who have children in the Brasstown Elementary School. While they were uncertain about what to do, they did share a belief that with some planning and positive action, the negative impact of the changes might be minimized. As they discussed their perceptions of the situation, they were poignantly aware that none of them had the viewpoint of the new housing project residents. They decided to involve representatives from the project, and, in inquiring with the resident manager about how to select someone, discovered the resident manager was also concerned and had initiated some approaches to assisting new residents in their move into the project.

The second meeting was attended by the resident manager and three project residents. This group of nine people became the nucleus of an expanding group of persons who in various ways participated in an exciting change process in the Brasstown Community.

The Condition A in Brasstown was complex indeed. The planning group was quite aware that many economic and political factors over which they had no control were at work. They believed, though, that by working together they could possibly exercise some significant influence in the direction they wanted. They were particularly concerned about the effects of the neighborhood changes on young people. The resident manager was a person with many good instincts and previous experience in reducing the impact of neighborhood change. He became the leader of the group. Because he lived and worked in the heart of the neighborhood, he was almost always available.

A Brasstown Community Council was organized and sub-groups were established to focus on matters like education, recreation, housing, jobs, transportation and health. This council was able to call attention to needs in the Brasstown area that were being overlooked or given little emphasis by city government, various commissions and boards and planning groups.

While much activity occurred on these various fronts, with some success and many frustrations, several significant gains were achieved on behalf of the young people in Brasstown.

This area of the city, for example, had always been lacking in recreational opportunities. The sharp increase in the youth population made this need urgent; the new housing projects were built with little provision for the young people. The Brasstown Community Council organized a Youth Advisory Group through which the young people were able to participate in identifying their own needs and making recommendations. The youths prepared a petition which included a detailed proposal to the housing authority, the recreation commission and the school board for a comprehensive recreation program using facilities in the neighborhood. Media attention helped gain support for this impressive initiative from the young people and the youths who participated saw tangible results of their efforts. Equally important, adult decision makers knew the young people were full participants in the positive action.

The Prevention Formula was used on several fronts at the same time throughout this complex sequence of events. It helped the group to analyze each situation it confronted. It helped those involved set realistic goals. It also assisted them in identifying the persons with power to influence the way things were developing in Brasstown. Most importantly, it helped them outline the kinds of resources they needed and could obtain for achieving their goals.

Because of the complexity of the changes taking place, members of the group realized they needed a way of sorting through the many forces at work and using them in the best interests of the neighborhood. Thus, they discovered the meaning of the Prevention Formula.

THE PROJECT WORKSHEET

The second action planning model, the Project Worksheet, is a simple variation of management by objectives. It goes beyond the essential ingredients of change as described, though it is not as complex or detailed as some management planning processes are. A simplified version is suggested, since it is recommended that diverse community groups become involved in the prevention effort, and many people will not be familiar with this kind of systematic planning.

The Project Worksheet can be used in many ways. It can be an aid in program and organization development. It can give structure and purpose to a group's activity while providing a basis for evaluating results. The Project Worksheet can be used in relation to planning with an individual or a family, it can be used to develop a program component, or it can facilitate achieving a solution to a community problem.

As an organization development tool, several Project Worksheets describing different elements of an organization's program can serve as a comprehensive description of that program. In this application, each functional area of the organization would describe its own goals, tasks and activities, budgetary and resource needs, and evaluation design.

The Project Worksheet can assist in sound deployment of personnel resources, giving more purpose and clarity to task assignments. It can also help to define the resources outside an organization's budgeted capability that are needed to complete a task.

Importantly, the Project Worksheet provides for the development of an evaluation design for measuring the extent to which goals have been achieved. The emphasis on timetables and the intent to accomplish certain tasks by particular times helps give specificity to the process.

All in all, the Project Worksheet promotes goal-directed activity within a group or organization. It encourages the best possible use of resources, and it provides a basis for determining whether or not, or to what extent, the desired outcomes have been achieved.

The Project Worksheet, with a description of each section, is as follows:

THE PROJECT WORKSHEET

Project Focus _____ Date of Initiation _____

Project Coordinator _____ Date of Completion _____

I. Description of situation to be changed (Condition A).

(This is a clear description of the current condition, giving enough detail to provide an adequate basis for planning the change.)

II. Description of the desired outcome (Condition B).

(These statements provide the *goals* and *objectives* of the effort. A goal is a clear, specific statement or statements describing the end results or conditions to be sought. An objective is a description of a shorter-range condition to be achieved in pursuit of the goal. Both goals and objectives should be limited enough to be achievable in a realistic period of time. Deadlines are useful in developing goals and objectives. At best, they are stated in a way that makes it evident when they are achieved.)

III. Evaluation design.

(This includes a set of indicators which make it possible to determine to what extent the goals and objectives have been achieved. If steps I and II are carefully developed, the completion of the evaluation design is made easier. If the goals and objectives are unclear, evaluation will be difficult if not impossible.)

IV. Tasks and activities.

(This describes a set of specific steps that are to be taken to achieve the objectives and goals. A time frame is useful for planning and monitoring progress.)

V. Resources.

(This describes comprehensively the resources needed to carry out the tasks and activities, including personnel, space and facilities, travel, financial resources, volunteers, materials, special talents, etc.)

The Project Worksheet can be used to develop a very detailed work plan, or it is possible that as few as several sentences under each heading can give enough direction to complete a project effectively and successfully.

FORCE FIELD ANALYSIS

Force field analysis[8] is a well known systematic approach to problem analysis and action planning that was developed by Kurt Lewin, a social psychologist, in the 1940s. It is simple in concept and provides a framework that a diverse group of community people can use in their efforts to plan and implement prevention strategies.

According to the force field concept, the *status quo* of an existing condition is maintained by two kinds of forces which work against each other. These are called *driving forces* and *restraining forces*. These can be visualized simply as:

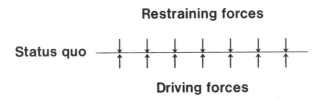

If the *status quo* is considered to be a situation that one wishes to change (Condition A), it is possible to analyze this condition in relation to these positive and negative forces. After determining a more desirable condition (the goal, or Condition B), it is then possible to consider how the positive, or driving, forces can be used and strengthened, and how the negative, or restraining, forces can be reduced or overcome to enable movement toward the goal. This change process can be visualized as follows:

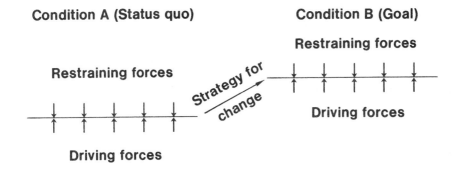

It is important to note that if and when Condition B is achieved, it will represent a new circumstance which will then be maintained by its own driving and restraining forces. This will need to be considered and planned for in order to assure that the continuing restraining forces do not cause a regression toward the former condition. In other words, the newly gained condition needs to be maintained and protected.

An outline for using force field analysis, such as the one that follows, can assist a group toward a clear action plan.

FORCE FIELD ANALYSIS

  I. Describe briefly the condition (Condition A) that is to be changed. Be very specific.

 II. Describe briefly the condition (Condition B) that is desired. Again, be very specific.

III. Describe briefly the existing positive or driving forces that will assist in moving from Condition A to Condition B.

IV. Describe briefly the existing negative or restraining forces that will impede moving from Condition A to Condition B.

 V. Review these lists and select those forces which, realistically, can be modified or used to promote the desired change.

VI. Briefly outline some action steps that will strengthen the driving forces that were selected.

VII. Briefly outline some action steps that will reduce or minimize the strength of the restraining forces.

VIII. Review these action steps and list the resources needed (human, physical, financial) to carry out the action.

IX. Place the action steps in logical order to make a rational and realistic action plan.

 X. Consider a plan for evaluating progress from Condition A to Condition B. (If steps I and II have been completed specifically and carefully, developing an approach for monitoring, describing and/or measuring progress toward Condition B need not be difficult.)

A useful example for engaging a group in learning to use force field analysis is the desire of a person to stop smoking. If Condition A on January 1 is that a person smokes two packs of cigarettes a day and that Condition B is to be a non-smoker on July 1, the group can be asked to complete the remaining eight steps of the process. This will include a listing of the positive forces which will encourage our subject to attain the goal, a listing of the negative forces which will discourage attaining the goal, a selection of those forces which can be used or impacted realistically, an outline of action steps which will strengthen the driving forces and minimize or negate the restraining forces, a list of the resources needed to carry out the action and placement of the action steps in logical order. Evaluation will be related to such indicators as the number of cigarettes consumed throughout the period of planned change and following July 1.

Several books include useful discussions of force field analysis.[9] An excellent example of this process at work is described in an article, "Force Field Analysis Applied to a School Situation," found in *The Planning of Change*.[10] A high school faculty uses force field analysis to bring about significant change in their school.

As has been suggested, these three planning and action models can be used singly or in sequence. The Prevention Formula can be useful for the initial general planning, or "scoping the situation." The Project Worksheet can be used for refining a more detailed work plan. Force field analysis is useful for "trouble shooting" at the beginning and along the way as roadblocks are experienced. If the group of key allies can not only become familiar with these tools but also use them, the purposeful and economical use of resources can be maintained throughout the effort. Once they have learned the skills and gained confidence in them, the people involved can teach them to others. Numerous groups of young people and adults have used these tools as they worked together in the interest of prevention, and they are applicable to change processes in all four quadrants of human service activity.

Once introduced to the group, these tools can be put to immediate use, although using them may seem awkward at first. Some practice on simple situations in which change is desired can help build skill in using them.

THE YOUTH OPPORTUNITY PLANNING PROCESS (Part III)

Once the planning and action tools have been made available to the group and some initial practice in using them has been completed, it is possible to return to the Youth Opportunity Planning Process (YOPP). This involves taking the 10 factors identified by the group as being the most significant contributors to the problem of concern and dealing with them specifically and systematically.

In reviewing the list of factors, it may be desirable to link some of them together or modify the way they are worded, depending upon the nature of the list that was prepared. Remember, those general statements were to serve as "direction pointers." This stage of the YOPP can become a substantial effort toward comprehensive planning and action for prevention. One approach to using this part of the YOPP is to organize one or more task forces around selected factors to pursue a topic in depth.

GUIDE FOR THE YOUTH OPPORTUNITY
PLANNING PROCESS (Part III)

Consider each factor separately.

Step 1

List those organizations, programs and individuals in the community who have demonstrated an active concern about this factor or who have a legal responsibility related to it.

Step 2

How many of these can you link together as working in a planned, systematic and collaborative manner to impact this factor significantly? Describe the linkages.

Step 3

Identify those efforts in the past three years that have been "effective" or promising in relation to this factor in the community. Describe them briefly.

Step 4

What important negative considerations tend to make this factor persist as a contributor to youth problems?

Step 5

Is there in the community a conscious and consistent policy related to this factor? If so, describe. If not, why not?

Step 6

Develop a list of key allies for bringing about specific change in relation to this factor. (Use the three-step strategy for this.)

Step 7

Develop a community action plan to bring about specific change in relation to this factor. (Use the Prevention Formula, the Project Worksheet or force field analysis, or a combination of them, to develop the plan.)

Obviously, to carry out these steps and to develop, implement and follow through on action plans related to even one of the factors calls for a serious commitment to discovering the meaning of prevention. In order to test the workability of this kind of community change process it must first be tried. Being aware of the numerous obstacles which might stand in the way is no small part of the challenge at this stage. Indeed, as one looks for allies it may appear that those persons who might be expected to become involved are the ones who most resist the changes being sought. At this point the strength of the Survival/Maintenance Mode is often encountered most forcefully. Here, too, is where the strength gained through carefully selected key allies becomes so crucial to the task of prevention.

It was stated at the beginning of this book that the intent is not to prescribe "answers" or "programs" for prevention, but rather *to equip people with practical concepts, strategies and tools through which they can determine their own paths, achieve their own results and gauge their own progress.* The kind of developmental process that is being advocated will require certain skills at all points along the way. One of the important aspects of engaging key allies is to identify people with the needed skills and, if possible, to gain their participation. If the needed skills do not exist, then it will be necessary to develop them. This, obviously, will take time. There can be a considerable amount of "learning through doing." In most communities there exist many talents that can be discovered through the kind of open exploration that occurs through a developmental process.

The author was involved several years ago with an "Inventory of Youth Opportunities" in a southeastern community. A lot of energy went into building information about the community in a variety of ways. The results were quite valuable, and the report of the study proved to be useful to a number of people and organizations in the community. It occurred to those involved, however, that the techniques used could be improved upon, and contact was made with members of the marketing research department of a large corporation in the city. Discussions with these technically skilled people revealed that they routinely used in their work a variety of techniques and methods that could be directly applied or easily adapted to making youth opportunities more relevant and attractive to the community's young people. These techniques had to do primarily with involving consumers in the development of ideas about the products they would purchase. (It seems at times that industry has more respect for its consumers than do human service organizations!) Had these industrial resource people been engaged in our inventory at an earlier stage, the initial work could have been made even more valuable.

Skills for prevention are not developed overnight. It takes time to encourage a prevention focus and to build the capacity to carry out the service options that prevention requires. Only a sustained effort over time will foster the accumulation of success and experience that will help to make prevention through positive community change a part of a community's practical knowledge and ongoing commitment.

AVENUES FOR BROAD CITIZEN INVOLVEMENT

Because this concept of prevention is an open community process that invites participation, it is important that there be a variety of avenues through which people can contribute their talents. The word avenue in this sense means simply "a means of accomplishing a purpose." The method of engaging key allies is one approach to identifying resource people, generating community involvement and recruiting talent.

There are several reasons for generating broad community involvement for a systematic process of planned community change. First, there are a variety of tasks to be accomplished, and talent is needed to do this well. Second, widespread participation can encourage a sense of ownership and vested interest in the change being sought, providing community sanction for the goals and methods of the prevention effort. Third, increased community education occurs as more people become involved. This can have a cumulative effect over time as people become exposed to a prevention perspective.

Another way to develop ideas for generating citizen involvement is a simple "brainstorming" activity. Brainstorming is a technique for quickly eliciting ideas from a group of people, without any discussion, elaboration or judgment of the validity of the ideas. Refinements come later. A question for starting the activity is, "How many avenues, methods or roles can you think of for involving people usefully in a prevention effort?" As ideas are suggested they are written, as stated, before the group. A challenge to the group might be to build a list of 15 or more avenues in 10 minutes or less. While it takes only a few minutes to prepare an initial list of a dozen or more ideas, this list can be expanded over time as people think of additional possibilities. It also can serve as a reminder to those involved of the variety of methods at their disposal for bringing others into the process as active and productive participants.

Examples of the kinds of ideas that emerge are as follows:

1. Policy group membership
2. Advisory group membership
3. Paid staff roles
4. Voluntary staff roles
5. Consultant
6. Technical advisor
7. Trainer
8. Assessment team member
9. Evaluator
10. Lobbyist
11. Interviewer
12. Respondent to surveys (consumer, opinion, etc.)
13. Advocate
14. Workshop participant
15. Community educator
16. Neighborhood task group member

When a group of young people and adults focus this task on a consideration of youth involvement in prevention, it becomes apparent that young people can in reality carry or participate in any role that an adult can carry. When these kinds of roles are designed into a goal oriented prevention plan, they can become viable and substantial ways to achieve the desired results. When prevention efforts are designed for specific community areas, such as schools or neighborhoods, the methods become more specific as they are planned to accomplish particular parts of the action plan.

While this emphasis might seem elementary and all too obvious, the unfortunate fact is that people are often excluded from meaningful participation in matters that are important to them and to which they can make positive contributions. The common practice of excluding young people from participation in the planning, operation and evaluation of opportunities that exist for their well-being is a case in point. An imaginative action plan related to youth development could well include young people in any or all of the 16 roles listed above.

MAINTAINING COMMUNITY SUPPORT

Three aspects of a prevention effort's relationship to the larger community are its *visibility,* its *credibility* and its *efficacy.* These three characteristics are important for generating and maintaining community support.

Visibility relates to *the general and specific awareness people in the community have of the prevention effort's goals, methods and accomplishments.* This awareness is best gained through tangible achievement, though it can be promoted through community education, efforts to generate community involvement and specific approaches to selected individuals and groups who need to know about the effort.

Because prevention invites community participation, increased visibility is a natural part of the prevention strategy. There is good potential for a well designed, positive prevention process to have a "snowball" effect. Word gets around quickly when something exciting is happening, and others tend to want to come and join the action.

Credibility is *the confidence people have in the effort and the capacity of those involved in it as an important and necessary undertaking in the community.* As with visibility, credibility is best gained through sound and convincing design and solid accomplishment in the area chosen by those responsible for the effort.

The basis of credibility in a prevention effort rests in large measure in the ability to engage those for whom the problem being dealt with is important and those who can exercise some control or influence over the conditions that need to be changed. The attitude undergirding a prevention effort is "let's work on this together." The building of confidence in the methods, strategies, leadership abilities and the quality of performance that are part of the prevention effort promotes high credibility.

Efficacy relates to *the ability to achieve tangible results in the accomplishment of the stated goals and objectives of the prevention effort.* Efficacy is best demonstrated through a program of evaluation which documents and confirms the outcomes of the effort, both intended and unintended. There is a good chance the efficacy of a prevention effort can be demonstrated if: (1) the goals are realistic and clearly stated, (2) the means for determining the extent to which the goals are achieved are designed into the strategy from the beginning, (3) the quality of information available accurately reflects the real situation, and (4) the necessary resources are available to carry out the evaluation.

Of these three aspects of a prevention effort's relationship to the larger community, efficacy is the most complex. Financial, technical and other resources needed for evaluation are seldom available, but evidence of efficacy needs constant emphasis if the benefits and validity of prevention are to be demonstrated.

Too often visibility, credibility and efficacy are left to chance rather than being managed with a sense of purpose. As all of the many complex parts of an effective prevention process come together, these concerns will be interrelated with many others. They should be kept in the forefront so they can receive the attention they deserve.

FOLLOWING THROUGH TO ACHIEVE RESULTS

The kind of serious and substantial developmental process that is being suggested as an approach to prevention does not occur without a concerted, sustained and committed community effort. Unless people are convinced that prevention is worthy of concentrated attention, commitment of resources and the personal and organizational energy needed to plan, initiate and carry through on such an effort, it will not happen.

Almost every community has in its recent experience examples of spirited, positive community action which has resulted in the achievement of some desired result. It may have been the attraction of a new industry, the building of a community center, the passage of a bond election, improvement of housing conditions or the formation of a new community orchestra or theater. Whatever it may have been, it undoubtedly required leadership, the personal commitment of key people, ownership among a sufficient number of people to assure the desired results and assertive follow-through to completion of the plan that had been adopted. No less is needed for successful prevention action.

For those who wish to undertake a prevention effort to bring about change in their community but lack a sense of direction, the ideas presented to this point provide a number of ways to begin and persist throughout their effort. The Community Development Workshop, as part of a prevention plan, can provide the setting and the stimulus to set such a process in motion.   □

chapter 6
Gauging Your Progress

When people commit their energy and resources to accomplishing some desirable goal, it is natural for them to want to know whether or not, or to what extent, their actions are successful. Even so, probably the most frustrating, least understood and most generally neglected aspect of human service activity is evaluation of results. Inadequate evaluation of human services has many causes. Funding sources, legislative bodies, policy groups, managers, practitioners, academic institutions that train professionals and evaluators themselves probably all contribute to the problem. Evaluation can be costly, raising issues about whether limited funds should go into services or efforts to evaluate them. The quality of evaluation results is often uneven, leaving program managers, policy groups and practitioners uncertain what they are getting for their money, or even that evaluation has benefits for them. When the community that supports public and private human service organizations is apathetic about the quality of service being rendered and does not demand accountability, it, too, may be contributing to the problem.

The *status quo* (Condition A) of most communities is that making those communities better places in which to live is not seen as "high technology." It is unlikely that in the near future we will see the technology of changing community conditions given the same value that we place on televisions and video games. This means research and development resources will probably not be available for changing the conditions that promote child abuse, delinquent behavior, mental health problems and other such symptoms that beset our communities. It means further that we will probably need to depend upon the good will and voluntary involvement of people who want to find ways to improve their communities. Fortunately, many such persons are currently working within the human service organizations of the community, and many more can be found in other places.

A key to how "successful" or how "effective" these people will be is directly related to their ability to *gauge their progress.* Gauging progress is a necessary part of any well designed change strategy, and the groundwork for this challenging task has been laid throughout the preceding chapters. It has been suggested that if a group of people interested in change are able to describe a current condition in clear and specific terms and then to describe clearly, realistically and practically a desirable outcome toward which they will work, it is then possible to establish some indicators of the extent they have moved from where they are to where they want to be. This, essentially, is what gauging progress is all about.

There are some practical ways that people involved in local prevention efforts can gauge their progress. The ideas that follow are presented with several purposes in mind. First, it is useful for the people involved to have a clear understanding of what is and is not possible in the way of evaluating the results of their efforts. Second, it is helpful to know some of the basic requirements of an evaluation effort. Third, it is possible for indicators of progress to be built into a prevention effort, even when sophisticated technical know-how and the funds to purchase it are not available.

WHY GAUGE PROGRESS?

In his book, *Developing Attitude Toward Learning*, Robert F. Mager presents the following dialogue.

"You can't measure the effects of what I do."

"Why not?"

"They're intangible."

"Oh, why should I pay you for intangible results?"

"Because I've been trained and licensed to practice."

"Hmm... all right. Here's your money."

"Where? I don't see it."

"Of course not... it's intangible."[11]

It is disconcerting that although human service activities may have been *assumed* to produce particular results, those activities may either not be getting those results, or, worse, may be promoting negative consequences. Actually we often do not really know the effects of many of our routine service activities because their results have not been evaluated.

In an article entitled "So Who's Interested in Results? A Skeptic's View of Evaluation of Youth Services,"[12] Thomas D. Bird makes some observations about the current status of evaluation that may well encourage us to gauge our progress.

Pointing out that doctors take pride in cures and carpenters in sound construction, he notes that those who serve youth are more likely to claim "special, personal concern for their clients" than to cite successful results of their efforts. The concern, however, is not enough.

Bird cites a study by Shorr and others of the National Center for Assessment of Delinquency and Its Prevention, who conducted an extensive search for evaluations of school-based delinquency prevention programs.

> They were able to find only 11 evaluations which (1) provided enough information to allow them to judge the adequacy of the research design and (2) used at least one measure which had some face validity as an index of delinquent behavior. The authors then assessed the research designs used in these evaluations. As a standard, they used a classic, widely used experimental research text (Campbell and Stanley, *Experimental and Quasi-Experimental Designs for Research*), which identifies a number of threats to the validity of research and proposes research designs to deal with them. The authors considered only four of the most common threats to validity. They concluded that "no evaluation's research design was able to control for a majority of these threats. As a result, it is *impossible to attribute claims of effectiveness to the programs' intervention strategies,* and we must conclude that we cannot know about the effectiveness of these programs because of the shortcomings of their evaluations." (Emphasis added.)

These conclusions were confirmed by other authors at the Assessment Center, who were able to make use of only nine of 52 evaluations of drug abuse prevention programs. Bird also cites Dennis Romig's report in *Justice for Our Children,* a review of evaluations of delinquency programs. Romig found only 170 of 850 evaluations to appear of sufficient quality to review. Most youth programs, Bird observed, "begin and end, or persist and multiply, without benefit of the scrutiny which rigorous evaluation would provide." Worse, some of Romig's findings of evaluations of delinquency programs indicated that, far from being beneficial, some youth services were either ineffectual or actually harmful:

- Nine of the evaluations were of projects using casework to reduce delinquency; 2,700 youths were involved. Results were conclusively negative for all nine projects. One project achieved a reduction in truancy among its clients, and one apparently produced significantly *more* police referrals and school disciplinary problems for those treated. None of the rest showed significant differences between treatment and control subjects in offenses or on any other outcome measure.

- Ten evaluations were of psychotherapy programs involving 1,600 young people. For seven of the 10 projects, outcomes for treatment and control groups were not significantly different. In one project, treatment subjects achieved better school performance and attendance and fewer probation referrals, but no reduction in police contacts. In another, youths who had been classified as "amenable" to the treatment achieved better parole performance, while those classified as "nonamenable" had slightly worse parole performance than controls. In the tenth project, the only difference was that those treated did slightly worse than controls on academic performance.

- In 28 group counseling programs for 1,800 young persons, one-fifth of the evaluations showed positive behavior changes in the subjects; in four-fifths, there were either no significant differences or negative results.

- Of 16 academic education projects, four reported on outcomes for delinquency. Only one of the four showed favorable results for the experimental subjects on measures of delinquency. Four of the 16 projects produced improvement in performance in at least one academic subject, while one improved school attendance. The other 12 projects, including the one that showed reduced delinquency rates, showed no significant differences in academic achievement.

- Of 14 behavior modification projects involving 2,000 youths, 10 of the 14 produced improvements of very narrow scope, but these did not transfer outside the treatment setting.

- In 12 family treatment programs involving 2,000 youths, four of the programs produced an apparent decrease in delinquent behavior in the treatment groups, five showed no effect, and three showed an apparent *increase* in delinquent behavior in the treatment groups.

- In 12 vocational and work programs, only three showed any effect on delinquency.

Other negative findings to which Bird referred include those reported by Dixon and Wright *(Juvenile Delinquency Prevention Programs)* for case-work, psychotherapy and group counseling as delinquency programs, and Ahlstrom and Havighurst *(400 Losers)*, about work programs in the 1960s. A Rand evaluation *(Federal Programs Supporting Educational Change)* for the U.S. Office of Education of efforts toward school innovation found "No class of existing educational treatments that consistently leads to improved student outcomes (when variations in the institutional setting and non-school factors are taken into account.)" Janvier and others of the National Center for Assessment of Delinquency and Its Prevention reviewed 52 evaluations of drug abuse prevention programs, half of which allowed no conclusions because of the inadequacies of design and many of which included no measure of drug abusing behavior. Nine programs used both an adequate evaluation design and a measure of drug abusing behavior; only four were found to be effective.

On the other hand, Bird noted that Janvier's review of drug abuse prevention program evaluations led the authors to conclude that "values-oriented" and "student participation alternatives" strategies appeared successful and warranted further examination. Similarly, four family therapy program evaluations that Romig reviewed apparently all taught parents "communication, problem-solving and disciplining skills." Evaluations can be quite useful in choosing and refining program strategies, but the utility of such evaluations depends greatly on their quality and number.

Bird concluded that, despite professed concern for young people, youth services will remain vulnerable to charges of uselessness at best or gross negligence at worst until adequate evaluation becomes the rule rather than the exception. Only then will there be defensible findings to confirm the effectiveness of programs that work and encourage abandonment of those that are ineffective or actually harmful.

Prevention initiatives which invite community participation will need to base their credibility upon a reasonable certainty that the strategies used are sound, have clear objectives and are capable of either achieving their intended results or can produce significant other outcomes that make them worthwhile in specific ways.

Some approaches to promoting change in all four arenas of human service activity will be based upon sets of assumptions that have yet to be tested through rigorous evaluation. To a large extent that is true of the strategies suggested in this book. While experience strongly indicates that positive results are obtained in limited areas of application, and while some of the change processes have been evaluated in areas such as organizational change, we have only begun to scratch the surface as regards the application of sound research methods to work in the prevention quadrants.

As efforts to discover the meaning of prevention are pursued, a worthy goal is the commitment of adequate research and evaluation resources to assessing the effectiveness of positive community development strategies for creating conditions that promote the well-being of people. Advocates of prevention are needed to pursue that goal, both for the compilation of existing studies about change which can provide insight and clarity to guide the process of discovery and for new financial and other resources for undertaking new studies. Economic conditions, the political atmosphere and human service systems heavily weighted toward remediation would seem to discourage strong moves in that direction at the present time. These realities notwithstanding, there are some important steps that can be taken by those concerned about prevention.

It would be encouraging to be able to say that the future belongs to those committed to demonstrating that their methods are effective, but we have a long way to go in human service endeavors and many obstacles to overcome before we get to that point. Even small steps toward this commitment can make a significant contribution, though, and each effort to gauge the progress of prevention initiatives, however limited their scale, is significant.

THE KEY TO GAUGING PROGRESS IS GOOD PLANNING

In Chapter II it was suggested that a well-planned prevention initiative goes through three stages: I. Orientation, Training and Planning; II. Implemtation and System Impact; III. Proof and Expansion. Each of these stages places emphasis on the importance of gauging progress. Careful documentation of each stage of the initiative becomes valuable in several ways, as will be shown.

A useful statement about evaluation is the following:

> The purpose of program evaluation is: *to determine the operations and effects of a specified program – relative to the objectives it set out to reach – in order to contribute to the decision-making surrounding the program.*[13]

This statement points in a helpful direction, whether the "specified program" is a huge multi-million dollar effort or a modest attempt by a family or a neighborhood group to promote change of some sort. Whatever the scope of the effort, it will include *doing something* ("operations") that, it is expected, will have some *intended results* ("effects...relative to the objectives it set out to reach") and for which someone is exercising some judgement and *taking responsibility* ("the decision-making surrounding the program").

A program which has a clear and direct relationship between its intended results, its strategies and the decision-making processes which give it direction has some of the characteristics of a well-planned approach. Another dimension of planning is the conceptual base, the assumptions or the theory which underlies the program. It was stated earlier that the Community Development Workshop is designed to equip people with concepts, strategies, tools and skills needed for a prevention initiative. The logical arrangement of these elements will enable a group of people to proceed in a systematic manner, and gauging progress becomes quite possible.

In reality, any set of circumstances that can be described in clear terms can become the basis of contrast or comparison with another set of circumstances. Previous chapters have suggested a number of ways that a prevention initiative can be undertaken by focusing attention on such matters as factors which contribute to the problems of people; the use of specific incidents, or "occasions for action," as starting points; specific symptoms that concern people; the status of youth participation in the community's youth-serving organizations; the processes through which decisions about resources are made; an examination of the forces which shape organizational design and the broader policy framework which exists in the community. All of these considerations tend to overlap and become intertwined with one another, presenting a complex and usually contradictory picture for those concerned about prevention. It is possible, though, to consider them systematically, to describe them, to plan changes related to them, and to gauge the progress made in relation to them. Again, the key to this is the ability to describe in clear terms the current condition (Condition A) and to describe a realistic, more desirable condition (Condition B) toward which people can work. The development of indicators of change related to these two conditions becomes the basis for gauging progress.

The measurement of change, in a real sense, is a political process. That is to say that it has to do with decision-making at the policy, management and service levels, and it can affect people (supporters, providers, recipients and participants) in a variety of ways. In the section on organizational lifestyles in Chapter III the following statements were used, and they relate to the political nature of evaluation. These statements represent the extremes of a range of attitudes toward evaluation, and the actual attitudes found in most communities probably lie somewhere between these extremes.

The Service Mode	The Survival/ Maintenance Mode
Evaluation of organizational effectiveness is seen as essential for improving services. Evaluation is an integral part of program management and necessary for accountability to the community which supports the organization.	Evaluation of organizational effectiveness is given little emphasis because it may point up change that is needed or even lead to questions about the validity of the organization's existence.

Understanding of the political realities that surround evaluation can be an important part of a change process and is directly related to the kind of planning necessary for gauging progress. Since prevention often challenges the *status quo*, evaluation can become a significant part of the change process itself. In fact, if evaluation is taken seriously, it can become a basis for direct impact on negative conditions and can help to create more positive conditions that promote the well-being of people.

As an example, consider a public recreation organization which, for the past several years, has been carrying out an unimaginative program that is essentially unattractive to people. An evaluation of the organization makes this condition quite clear and actually demonstrates that staff members have been actively alienating the people of the neighborhood. On the basis of the evaluation, policy decisions are made which lead to program and staff changes. The result is a greatly revised use of the recreation center, a new program that is attractive to people and a new condition which clearly benefits the neighborhood in a number of ways. This kind of change process, which can be both initiated and described by evaluation, is obviously one that creates new conditions which enhance the well-being of people in the community.

Efforts to document, describe and analyze what takes place throughout a prevention initiative can help to give the initiative direction, keep it on course and, if the results are positive, encourage those responsible to persist in their efforts. Documented success also helps to establish the validity of the strategies and methods used and encourages those involved to use their skills and energies in other ways to better their community. Conversely, and equally important, if the evaluation indicates that the effort is not succeeding or is having negative, unintended results, there is basis for stopping what is happening.

When the value of gauging progress is recognized from the beginning and attention is given to it in practical, realistic and manageable ways, the people responsible will be rewarded with useful information about what they are doing.

FIVE EVALUATION LEVELS
FOR GAUGING PROGRESS

Distinguishing among five levels of evaluation helps to determine what is possible in gauging progress and encourages a realistic emphasis on evaluation in a prevention initiative. This framework also helps those responsible for planning the prevention effort to maintain evaluation as a focus of attention because it is seen as integral to the management of the initiative. (See note below.)

These five levels of evaluation begin with the simplest and build to more complex levels. To some extent, each level builds upon the preceding one.

Note – The author, who does not possess the technical skills of research evaluation, is indebted to Peter S. Venezia, Ph.D. for many of the ideas included in this section.

The questions raised at each level and the need for documentation can enhance the relevance of the strategies used in the prevention initiative.

Level 1 – Monitoring

Monitoring consists of the collection of data relevant to the activities of the program. It focuses upon the questions, "How much?" and "How many?" Decisions will need to be made about what kind of information to collect in order to document the current condition the group is concerned about. The information generated at this level can serve as baseline data to be used later for comparison. Depending upon the nature of the situation, there may be a considerable amount of information readily available, or it may be necessary to generate new data.

To illustrate, consider the example of the school principal concerned about the amount of vandalism in the school. Information about the number of broken windows over the past several years would be useful to show recent trends. Other indicators of the current condition can be added to this. If it is suspected that the feeling of alienation from the school among the students might be a factor, an opinion survey or a study of the number and quality of opportunities students have to participate in decisions about the school could produce useful information for later comparison. The group involved in describing the current condition will be able to generate a number of ideas about the situation which can suggest the kinds of information that will be useful. As the planning stage of this initiative gets under way, and even after implementation of the strategy, additional ideas about useful information will come into focus.

The need for monitoring continues throughout the initiative. In addition to the indicators that have been selected as important to the change being sought, monitoring can focus on the administration of internal organizational matters such as fiscal management, staff deployment, time usage, the consumption of supplies, etc. Monitoring can be as simple or as complex as need be to serve the purposes of sound management and gauging progress.

Level 2 – Process Description

This level of evaluation focuses upon a description of the strategies and methods used in an effort to bring about the desired change. The basic questions at this level are "Who does what when?" "Under what circumstances?" "For what reasons?" The emphasis here is to capture in narrative description those matters that are dynamically related to the change being sought. The task of describing will of necessity engage those involved in considering what is important about what they are doing and asking if they are doing the right things to get from Condition A to Condition B. The entire process of gauging progress encourages more incisive, critical thinking about the use of resources for change and the methods being used to achieve it.

The documents prepared at this level of evaluation can be circulated among all of the key allies involved in the initiative to get reactions and sharpen the group's collective ideas about why they are doing what they are doing. As this level is related to monitoring and to the levels to follow, a self-correcting approach to bringing about the desired change can take shape.

To continue the illustration about vandalism in the school, the group of people responsible for designing and implementing the strategy would find it useful, as their strategy takes shape, to describe it in specific detail. This will help to relate their activities both to their Condition A and Condition B descriptions and to the kinds of things they decided to monitor at level 1. A part of this documentation will include the sequence of events that take place over time as the group moves through its program of planned change. Obviously, much learning can be derived from this. The survey methods used to elicit student opinion about the conditions in the school, the experiences the surveyors have as they talk with people, the relationship of the policy group (school board) to the process, what is done with the results of the survey and other such matters will be useful parts of the process description.

Sensitivity to other matters that might influence the outcome of the change strategy is important. As the group begins to consider what they are doing as it relates to what they hope to achieve, members become more aware of pertinent outside factors and better able to identify the various forces with which they will need to contend. A process description of their methods and implementation of them can encourage them to think about these factors.

At this level, evaluation provides a record of everything being done to achieve the desired results. This history will be useful in a number of ways, including the documentation of successful prevention activity, if the effort does in fact succeed. If the documentation is clear, concise and to the point, it need not be long or require a burdensome effort.

Level 3 – Outcome Enumeration

This level of evaluation focuses upon what happened in relation to the relevant indicators in the move from Condition A to Condition B. Because baseline data will have been established at the monitoring level, it will be possible to determine some outcome measures at various times throughout the initiative. These points could be during the effort, at a specified completion date, or at a time after the project is over.

It is important to emphasize that while work at this level, if done well, can indicate what has happened after a certain time, *it cannot specify what relation the program described at level 2 had to the outcome, if any.* In other words, if pre-program baseline data have been collected, comparisons can be made to determine through-time changes. Such changes, either positive or negative, cannot, however, be attributed strictly to the program. They might have occurred in the absence of the program, or in spite of it. An examination of the direct relationship between program and outcome requires more stringent methods of evaluation, specifically those related to the next level.

In our example, it will be easy to determine any changes in the rate of broken windows at the school. It may be more difficult to develop more subtle indicators of outcome. These might include changes in levels of alienation from the school, self-concept of students, attitudes of teachers, administrators and policy board members, etc. If a Quadrant 3 program of community problem solving focusing on the amount of destructive behavior and its reduction has been undertaken, the evaluation task may not be too difficult. If, however, a Quadrant 1 initiative to create conditions which promote the well-being of people is the intent, Condition B will be described in different terms, and additional indicators beyond the number of broken windows will be useful.

The selection of indicators to which outcome measures will be attached can be a constructively provocative undertaking for students, teachers, administrators and policy board members. This can probe deeply into the mission of the school and how all aspects of the school are related to that mission. The symptom of vandalism, then, can become an "occasion for action" that serves as a beginning point for a broader experience in organizational renewal. The task of measuring the outcomes of the program of planned change in the school can become a key aspect of a community development process.

The development of outcome measures for any kind of prevention initiative helps keep key allies clearly focused upon the results in which they are interested. Close attention to this level of evaluation, therefore, is an integral part of the overall effort.

It should be observed that most evaluation of human service efforts goes only to this level. It is not uncommon for human service organizations, in their annual reports and other documents, to claim that their program was responsible for the outcome, especially if that outcome is positive. There is, however, little justification for such a claim if the evaluation effort stopped here. There may be apparent relationships between the program and the outcome, but if the evaluation did not go further, an honest appraisal will indicate that the claim to "success" is only speculative.

Level 4 – Measurement of Effectiveness

This level of evaluation answers the difficult question: *What would have happened in the area of the program's operation had the program not been available?* In a remedial program which has a client group, one approach to this evaluation task is to use control groups. In a condition-focused, Quadrant 1 prevention effort, however, evaluation at this level is a different challenge. It requires a set of circumstances similar enough to the program "target" to provide valid comparisons with which to determine the impact of the program. Then the evaluator can be reasonably sure of what would have happened had the program not existed. A careful analysis of external factors which might affect the outcome of the program is essential at this level.

In our school vandalism example, if there are two schools which are similar in program, symptoms, neighborhood characteristics and other factors, and if these two schools enter into an effort to test the validity of prevention strategies, one can be used for the experimental program while the other maintains its existing program. Then it may be possible to construct an evaluation design which can go to the level of measurement of effectiveness. Such controlled circumstances would elicit very useful information about the validity of prevention strategies. The need for a carefully constructed evaluation design is obvious. The technical requirements for such an evaluation are quite stringent, calling for substantial resources, both technical and financial.

It is unfortunate that human service endeavors are seldom evaluated at this level, but there are many reasons why, not the least of which are cost and the availability of the required technical know-how.

Level 5 – System Impact

This level goes beyond the actual effects of the program upon individuals or upon specific program targets to determine impact upon systems or conditions within which the program target is imbedded. This impact can be a part of the intended results of the program, or Condition B, if there is a conscious effort to create a "ripple effect" through the initiative.

In our example, if the immediate concern is the reduction of vandalism and the changing of conditions related to the vandalism, there are potentially a number of system considerations that can be addressed indirectly, if not directly, through the prevention initiative. If a high level of alienation of students from the governance process of the school is related to the vandalism, the program to be instituted may seek to introduce various approaches to student involvement in that process, expecting that a number of system changes might occur. These could include student involvement in shaping curriculum and discipline policy, peer counseling, and other key aspects of the life of the school. A kind of system impact, then, might be that teachers find they spend less time and energy in disciplinary matters and have more time for classroom instruction. The change in attitude toward students as resources in the school could open other doors not anticipated. If the atmosphere in the school becomes more positive and students feel more ownership in the quality of that atmosphere, there could be unanticipated change in attendance, achievement, and other indicators of the quality of the school's climate. Increased attendance could attract more state funds, higher achievement levels could attract more college scholarships for students, and teacher and administrator morale might improve. All of these outcomes are part of the impact of the program on the system. A well-planned evaluation will be mindful of these potential outcomes and accommodate them when they occur.

Two additional levels that might be considered are societal impact and new knowledge. The ultimate purpose of research evaluation is the advancement of knowledge. Discoveries that develop to the point that they have broad societal impact take on the significance of what Marilyn Ferguson calls a "paradigm shift."[14] Indeed, it would be a grand accomplishment if human services were to shift from a remedial, reactive mindset to one oriented toward wellness and the promotion of positive conditions. Such a shift would have significant societal impact.

DETERMINING THE QUALITY OF EFFORTS TO GAUGE PROGRESS

In addition to the five levels of evaluation, four critical factors can determine the nature and quality of the evaluation process. These are (a) the quality of goals and objectives, (b) the quality and availability of relevant data, (c) the quality and adequacy of the resources available for evaluation, and (d) the congruence of expectations held by various key people about the evaluation task.

Much has already been said about the importance of clear Condition A and Condition B statements that specifically describe the beginning and ending points of the prevention initiative. If goals and objectives do not describe clear and measurable outcomes, evaluation beyond the process description level will be difficult if not impossible. The lack of stated, measurable goals is probably one of the greatest weaknesses in human service programs. The adequacy of the description of the desired outcome of the prevention initiative provides a clear criterion for evaluating the initiative.

A second criterion, the quality and availability of relevant data, flows from the first. The determination of what data are needed is obviously related to indicators of progress from Condition A to Condition B. The quality of these data is often determined by the attitudes of those who produce or guard the data and their commitment to the evaluation process. The shaping of the evaluation design and the construction of its necessary ingredients depend in large measure upon the forthrightness of the questions asked and the willingness of key actors in the situation to have those questions answered. The guardians of existing information that can become useful in a prevention initiative may be located in several organizations under different administrations. A cooperative approach is the starting point. Fragmented service systems may lack the capacity to produce relevant data that are of consistently high quality. The challenge to create ways to generate the needed data and to assure their quality is one that prevention initiators will have to meet if valid evaluation is to be achieved.

The quality and adequacy of the resources available for evaluation can also determine the nature of evaluation. Technical knowledge and skill and the financial resources to purchase them are immediate needs. This is especially true if the desire is to achieve the more complex levels of evaluation and when the situation being dealt with is complicated. Other needed resources may include personnel and equipment. Even when the other two criteria are adequately met, if adequate resources are not available, useful evaluation is unlikely to occur.

The other critical factor is the congruence of expectations about the evaluation task held by various key people. Depending upon the nature and scope of the prevention initiative, this may become a source of real frustration for the people involved. If the effort requires cooperation among several organizations and funding has been obtained from public or private sources, several groups of people will have legitimate expectations about the evaluation of the initiative. The policy, management and service delivery groups of the participating organizations each can use evaluation results. Similarly, an involved citizen group has its own interest in outcomes, as do the funding sources and the core leadership group for the initiative. Representatives of these varied groups are unlikely to meet to make clear and informed decisions about the level of evaluation that is desirable. This means that it is unlikely that there will be a planned, agreed-upon approach to evaluation, and discrepancies in expectations about evaluation can become a problem. Too often one group's expectations, usually those of the funding source, determine the nature of the evaluation effort, and the result is that required reports are not integrated into a well-planned evaluation approach which serves the purposes of the key allies doing the work.

Ideally, the planning process for evaluation will be based upon a clear determination of what kind of evaluation will best support the achievement of the initiative's goals, with all expectations focused on that concern. It is obvious that "getting it all together" to evaluate a prevention initiative will challenge the dedication of any group of people. Does this mean, then, that some modest and useful attempts to gauge the progress of the initiative will inevitably run into insurmountable difficulties? Not necessarily. What this brief review of the nature of evaluation can do is help a group of people proceed on a realistic basis so they do not defeat themselves by their own unrealistic expectations.

Several observations may lend encouragement. First, a group of people may not be as much interested in a scientific analysis of what gets results as in seeing certain results achieved. This can mean that trying to measure effectiveness would surpass their capacity, while outcome enumeration would give them the assurance they need that their efforts are moving in an acceptable direction. The third level is certainly easier, less technical and costly, and requires fewer resources than going to level four. This consideration alone can encourage the group to determine a realistic level of evaluation without sacrificing the credibility of their efforts.

Second, because a prevention effort is developmental in nature, and often quite exploratory, it is possible to begin with some rather simple monitoring, with a view toward learning some things that will help the entire effort, including the evaluation, grow in a planned and purposive manner. This growth process can include developing the technical capacity for evaluation.

Third, since the kind of community participation process being suggested depends upon key allies working together in a positive manner, the effort can be designed and facilitated to assure, insofar as possible, that the keepers of needed information are included in the process. The same applies to those who have the technical skills needed for evaluation. These resources can often be found within the community, or at least the region, where the initiative is taking place.

Figuring out how to build the capacity to do useful and appropriate evaluation is like solving any other problem. The task can be approached in a planned and systematic manner. It can help to describe the Condition A of the group's ability, determine what the Condition B of adequate evaluation needs to be, and then develop a work plan to achieve the desired result. The planning tools presented in Chapter V can be used for this purpose.

DESIGNING A MONITORING PROGRAM
FOR COMMUNITY DEVELOPMENT

A practical way to incorporate the various strategies and tools that have been presented into a comprehensive program of community development is to design and initiate a community monitoring program. Such an undertaking could be focused upon a specific interest area, such as young people or the elderly. Or it could be even more general. Using a focus on young people as an example, a group might begin with the Youth Opportunity Planning Process and shape a community monitoring program around the factors that are identified. Part III of the YOPP suggests a number of considerations that can be used as starting points. Additional planning through the use of the Prevention Formula, the Project Worksheet and force field analysis will generate many more ideas about the kinds of information that can be included.

It would be shortsighted, indeed, not to place emphasis upon using the technology and the tools of the "information society" in this endeavor. The resources for this are probably readily at hand in most localities. Most schools have microcomputers, many students learning to use them, and teachers who have the necessary skills for software development. Granting course credit to students can build the effort into the school curriculum. Private businesses also have equipment that is not in use after hours. A community volunteer effort to develop the computer programs needed and to make the technical know-how and necessary hardware available can be organized. Since youth participation is a necessary ingredient of any viable youth development endeavor, this will bring young people into key roles in all aspects of the effort. Since such an undertaking is related to the mission of almost all youth serving organizations, both public and private, staff time from these agencies will probably be willingly contributed.

Using the process to engage key allies will be important as the various kinds of information needed for the monitoring program are identified. Involving the keepers and collectors of that information is essential. Assuring that the process is shaped through a wide diversity of points of view is equally important. An effort built from the ground up and shaped by the people who become involved is likely to become engaging and refreshing to an expanding number of people.

As of this writing, the author is not aware of this kind of approach to a community monitoring system having been undertaken. Various approaches to "needs assessment" have been used, but they either tend to have an individual remedial, or Quadrant 4, flavor or they have been based upon a prescribed data collection procedure which does not involve people in the shaping of it. The results frequently sit on shelves with little utility.

A community monitoring program which is shaped and owned by the people of the community can serve as a positive, assertive way to determine what kind of community people want to live in and provide a basis for planning and action for moving more in that direction.

Is your community becoming what you want it to be, and how do you know? As people increasingly incorporate concern for gauging progress into their thinking processes they are likely to become more eager to get results, demonstrating that people can become responsible, within realistic limits, for shaping the conditions under which they live. □

chapter 7

Building A Support System For Prevention

Numerous favorable signs today encourage us to believe that prevention as a positive force will gain momentum and assume its proper role in the design of human service endeavors. In his book, *Megatrends: Ten New Directions Transforming Our Lives,* John Naisbitt identifies some significant shifts that are taking place in our society.[15] Almost all of these trends are directly related to the dynamics of prevention as they have been presented in the preceding chapters. He says we are moving from an industrial society to an information society, from "forced technology" to "high tech/high touch," from a national economy to a world economy, from short term to long term planning, from centralization to decentralization, from institutional help to self-help, from representative to participatory democracy, from hierarchies to networking, from north to south, and from either/or choices to multiple options. Naisbitt's richly illustrated discussion of these trends suggests that people are moving toward taking more responsibility for shaping the conditions which affect them. He cites numerous examples of people determining what they want and effectively and successfully joining forces to get the results they want. Interestingly, however, few of these examples come from the human service institutions and organizations of local communities; most are initiated outside the frameworks of established structures. If human service organizations tend to become even more reactive and remedial in a tight economy, they may need to learn from what is happening in the world around them.

In her discussion of the "paradigm shift," Marilyn Ferguson says that a paradigm is "a scheme for understanding and explaining certain aspects of reality.... A paradigm shift is a distinctly new way of thinking about old problems."

A new paradigm involves a principle that was present all along but unknown to us. It includes the old as a partial truth, one aspect of How Things Work, while allowing for things to work in other ways as well. By its larger perspective, it transforms traditional knowledge and the stubborn new observations, reconciling their apparent contradictions.

The new framework does more than the old. It predicts more accurately, and it throws open doors and windows for new exploration.

Given the superior power and scope of the new idea, we might expect it to prevail rather quickly, but that almost never happens. The problem is that you can't embrace the new paradigm unless you let go of the old. You can't be half-hearted, making the change bit by bit... The new paradigm is not "figured out" but suddenly seen.

New paradigms are nearly always received with coolness, even mockery and hostility. Their discoveries are attacked for their heresy. (For historic examples, consider Copernicus, Galileo, Pasteur, Mesmer.) The idea may appear bizarre, even fuzzy, at first because the discoverer made an intuitive leap and does not have all the data in place yet...

But the new paradigm gains ascendance. A new generation recognizes its power. When a critical number of thinkers has accepted the new idea, a collective paradigm shift has occurred. Enough people have caught onto the new perspective, or have grown up with it, to form a consensus. After a time that paradigm, too, is troubled by contradictions; another breakthrough occurs, and the process repeats itself. Thus science is continually breaking and enlarging its ideas.[16]

In human service endeavors we are sorely in need of a major paradigm shift from the strongly reactive, remedial mindset that dominates the current situation to an active, assertive prevention perspective which can open new possibilities for creating conditions that promote the well-being of people. The exciting reality is that the technology exists for us to make this shift – the question is whether or not we will commit ourselves to moving in that direction.

This book is built upon the optimistic premise that people are able to become responsible, within realistic limits, for shaping the conditions under which they live. This does not happen spontaneously and without effort. It happens by choice and requires systematic planning. It can happen with single individuals, but to be effective on a larger scale it requires that people come together in joint efforts of cooperative participation as they work toward mutually desirable results. This, at best, involves a conscious approach to building support systems to sustain them and guide their efforts.

Human service endeavors have, by and large, been designed from an individual remedial (or Quadrant 4) mindset. We have committed vast resources to maintaining institutions and organizations that are substantially locked into methods based upon the confines of that arena. If, indeed, we were to experience a major paradigm shift from a Quadrant 4 to a Quadrant 1 approach – one which has as its primary commitment the creation of conditions which promote the well-being of people – we would find that *new possibilities for more effective work can emerge in and through all four arenas of human service activity.*

Using Quadrant 1 as a beginning point has potential for enriching what happens in all four arenas of human service activity. Quadrant 1 activity promotes personal growth and development in that it recognizes each person as a resource; gives each person an opportunity to become involved in a meaningful, contributing role; prepares each participant with the needed concepts, strategies, tools and skills to make a positive contribution and focuses on creating conditions within which positive change can occur. Quadrant 1 activity provides an opportunity to go beyond the community problem solving thrust of Quadrant 3 and encourages a positive emphasis on proactively shaping conditions which are less likely to be in need of problem solving. Quadrant 1 activity also addresses many of the concerns of individual remediation, though it sees the individual more as an active participant, with others, in a positive experience of community change. In short, Quadrant 1 activity has a peculiar contribution to make to human service work and possesses qualities that do not exist in the other quadrants. Indeed, Quadrant 1 approaches can improve the conditions under which activity in the other three quadrants takes place. This suggests that placing more emphasis on Quadrant 1 can be a catalyst for transforming all kinds of human service endeavors.

Creating the right kind of atmosphere is a crucial step in discovering the meaning of prevention. Building a support system for prevention takes place at several levels, and the sections of this chapter which follow will examine the construction process, beginning with some relatively simple ideas about prevention as a group task and moving to more complex considerations focused upon organizing statewide initiatives.

PREVENTION AS A GROUP TASK

A strong emphasis has been that *key allies* are needed if a substantial prevention initiative is to be undertaken. Focusing on conditions makes it possible to promote desirable change. The sense of community through which this kind of change can occur depends upon groups of people who foster a *community development process.*

The selection of key allies is a purposive part of a prevention strategy. The positive engagement of people who have the needed skills and talents, people who can carry out the tasks of the action plan, and people who can exercise some control over the conditions to be changed is an essential aspect of the assertive approach this book describes. This becomes the basis, too, of people "buying into" and developing ownership of the goals, strategies and tasks of the prevention effort.

The kinds of service options described in Chapter II as belonging to a community development approach require a group effort. Each service option is both a group responsibility and a component of expanding group involvement and interaction.

Since a community development approach to prevention is, by its very nature, best approached as a group task, the challenge of building a support system requires attending to a variety of realities. Some of these realities, as discussed in earlier chapters, are negative forces that will impede the progress of those who would promote prevention. They include resistance to change among key people, dependence upon organizations whose prescribed structure comes from outside the community, strong tendencies toward the Survival/Maintenance Mode, heavy emphasis upon remediation, a lack of clear concepts of prevention, and confused or conflicting values and assumptions among those who would cooperate in the venture. Quite possibly these may be complicated by less than helpful constraints from state and federal levels.

On the more positive side, some of the driving forces which can encourage a prevention effort are the natural resources that people in the community represent, the desire and willingness of at least a few people who will commit themselves to the task, the availability of developmental tools and strategies which are easily understood and taught to others, an increasing awareness of the wisdom of using available resources to bring about community change, and a growing impatience among some people with the ineffectiveness of past methods. *A persistent attitude which utilizes these driving forces can do much to overcome or work around the restraints that exist, particularly if it happens within a supportive group environment.*

Even when key allies in a prevention initiative include some very experienced people, the stage must be properly set if the effort is to be successful. Following some basic rules can assist any group in carefully designing an effective strategy.

Start small and build upon success. As the first steps toward shaping a prevention initiative are taken, they can be modest, manageable steps that are reasonably certain to succeed. Discussion about the idea of the initiative with friends and colleagues will help to identify needed resource people who are interested. Building from the ground up in this manner helps to establish a comfort level which is important for those promoting the process, particularly in its earliest stages.

Practice communicating ideas about prevention with sympathetic people. Test them out first with people you know will listen and who will agree with you while being constructively critical. Discussing ideas in a caring and accepting atmosphere helps in developing a comfort level with concepts for sharing them with others. This might be done at first with a spouse, a close friend or a trusted colleague. This initial experimentation is good preparation for interchange with people who will challenge the ideas, disagree with them, or find them threatening.

Do a lot of personal emissary work. If members of the initial group proceed systematically to contact and talk with other selected people about the prevention initiative, it is possible to cultivate a group of key allies prior to ever bringing them together. These people can be contacted informally, one or two at a time, and sold on some of the concepts of prevention prior to their knowing they will be asked to become part of a carefully designed community development strategy. These conversations can occur over lunch, during recreation or during a personal visit. Careful groundwork can reap dividends at later points in the prevention process and interaction with potential allies can enrich the thinking of the members of the core group. Communication is a two-way, mutually beneficial exchange.

Listen to people's reactions and learn from them. If the people with whom group members talk represent a variety of viewpoints, they can provide valuable insights about the community, the problem that is of concern, various political realities and other important considerations.

Do not rush the process, but build systematically. Trying to move too quickly before the building blocks are in place can get the community change process off to a bad start or sabotage it completely. Impatience is one of the chief foes of an effective prevention program. Trying to force someone or a situation can often serve only to increase resistance. This does not mean that confrontation is not useful and often needed, but it should be used as part of a carefully designed strategy. When pursuing a change strategy that is directed toward the accomplishment of positive goals, it is possible to engage people in the pursuit of those goals. This takes time and it is important to be sensitive to the pace that others are able to handle. Patient persistence can help facilitate a successful prevention process.

Keep your expectations at a modest level and you are less likely to be disappointed. One of the contributing factors to personal "burn-out" in prevention efforts is the frustration and sapping of valuable emotional energy that comes from unmet, unrealistic expectations. It is, on the other hand, an energizing experience to be pleasantly surprised by small accomplishments. If the core group's expectations are geared to a level that even small steps and modest progress become sources of gratification and excitement, then it is more likely that the effort will be seen through to a positive conclusion. If this kind of satisfaction is shared by a group of people as the progress of the prevention program is assessed, it can be a source of mutual encouragement.

The experience of planning for and using an action strategy such as a Community Development Workshop can become the focus for the early stages of the prevention initiative. It can serve both to build cohesion in the group and to provide a forum for the shaping of the initial action steps. Further, it can equip people with the concepts, strategies and tools they need at all stages of the prevention initiative. Skill development comes through the application of the strategies and tools.

ADVOCACY AND TECHNICAL ASSISTANCE: TWIN FORCES FOR POSITIVE CHANGE

A primary purpose of a support system for prevention is to insure availability of new forces which have the strength, the influence and the sustained momentum to influence the conditions which need to be changed. These new forces exist primarily in the form of the human resources of the community — arranged, organized and equipped as they must be to carry out a prevention initiative. Two such forces that can become key resources in the prevention support system are *advocacy* and *technical assistance.*

Most people, either informally or professionally, participate in many forms of both, and they do it with regularity. These activities play important roles in our lives, but are seldom used positively to capitalize on their potential contribution to prevention. When used with purpose and skill, advocacy and technical assistance become twin forces for positive change.

Advocacy is defined as "an act of pleading for, supporting, or recommending; active espousal."[17] The word "advocate" (noun) is defined as "one who defends, vindicates, or espouses a cause by argument; upholder; defender; one who pleads for or in behalf of another; intercessor."[18]

Technical assistance is defined as *a process of providing to a person, group or organization supportive help that is focused upon some technical aspect of meeting a need, effecting a change, or achieving a goal.*

Only a moment's reflection is needed to realize that these two activities are extremely pervasive. Who has not argued some cause or advocated something with someone in the past day or two? Any time someone shares a new recipe or diet or makes suggestions about how to hold the golf club or improve the backswing, technical assistance is being provided.

What is advocacy as it relates to prevention? What is technical assistance? Are the two compatible? Can and should advocacy and technical assistance be attempted, encouraged and used within the framework of one particular strategy or organized effort? What are the implications of each for the other? Does one role tend to support, neutralize or undermine the other?

One of the problems in clarifying these processes and the activities related to them is that they overlap. It can be useful, even at the risk of overstating the differences, to distinguish between some of the qualities peculiar to each of these two important thrusts.

Advocacy, as most often experienced in the human service arena, has two common forms. The first is advocacy for specific individuals. This form would tend to fit with what has been described as a remedial, or Quadrant 4, activity. An example would be an advocate's going to a social agency with a person who does not understand the procedures of large organizations in order to help that person achieve eligibility for services or more efficient assistance.

The second kind of advocacy is for a cause or for changes in conditions which affect people. This is illustrated by advocacy for higher *per diem* payments for foster parents, removal of status offenders from the jurisdiction of the juvenile court, better educational opportunities for young people, or more adequate housing for elderly citizens. When applied to conditions that might be the focus of a prevention effort, this form of advocacy can be seen as part of a community development strategy.

With either of these forms, *advocacy is basically issue oriented.* It emanates from positions that are developed and promoted in specific ways. The advocate puts the position in the forefront and consciously creates a personal identification with that position.

The position is by nature value laden. Its purpose is to confront and persuade. Its benefit is the persuasiveness it carries and the impact it has on the thinking and behavior of others. Advocacy is usually directed toward individuals or groups who are in a position to effect specific changes or who are in control of specific situations.

Though new skills may be needed to effect the change being advocated, advocacy does not attempt to promote skill development. The advocate may or may not have the capacity to train others to develop those skills. Such capacity building is not a part of advocacy. This is the role of technical assistance.

By the way of contrast, *technical assistance is oriented toward skill development and toward techniques for facilitating specific changes to accomplish particular results.* Examples of technical assistance are helping a staff group shape organizational goals, assisting a policy board in developing ways to conduct more productive meetings, or helping a group of people develop a strategy to bring about a particular change in their neighborhood.

While the technical asistance provider has values which undergird the technical assistance relationship, the intent is not to persuade. The technical assistance provider does not put values and positions in the forefront. The relationship is focused on the identification of the user's needs and the shaping of specific strategies for meeting those needs. It is quite possible that the technical assistance provider and user have very different values, which need not interfere with the teaching of needed skills.

Both advocacy and technical assistance are ways of attempting to influence the thinking and behavior of others. From the point of view of the person or group being influenced, technical assistance usually is invited and wanted; advocacy may not be. For example, a school board may hold an open hearing on a particular problem to encourage citizen participation in the solution of that problem. When people come to advocate their positions, they are there because of open invitation. At other times, since school board meetings are public meetings, groups of people may come to advocate positions when not specifically invited. This uninvited advocacy may be directed toward change in policy or toward some aspect of how the schools are operated. The same school board may engage a consultant to provide technical assistance to focus on the same problems.

Another difference between the two is that advocacy is usually backed up by strong emotional appeal. Technical assistance is usually more dispassionate. The advocate feels more personally involved in the outcome of his or her efforts, while the skilled technical assistance provider recognizes the right and responsibility of the user to make a decision about the outcome. While the technical assistance provider is certainly interested in the outcome of the transaction, there is less of a feeling of personal involvement in the choice of the user.

People can become involved in both advocacy and technical assistance as volunteers or as paid professionals. There may be a tendency to think of advocacy as being a voluntary citizen role and technical assistance as a paid professional role. This is not necessarily true, however. Citizens can certainly carry the advocate role effectively. Professional persons often take strong advocacy positions too. At the same time, persons not involved in a particular arena professionally can provide valuable technical assistance.

There are at least four kinds of people who need to be engaged in building a support system of key allies for a prevention effort. These are (a) advocates, (b) technical assistance providers, (c) persons who are sources of insight about the conditions in need of changing and (d) controllers/influencers of those conditions. Both advocates and technical assistance providers are needed on a continuing basis as capacity for prevention is built over time. The sources of insight and controllers of specific conditions are called upon when their talents and resources are needed.

Effective advocacy helps to create an atmosphere which sanctions the positive goals of a prevention effort. It also uses persuasion to influence those who can control or influence the conditions to be changed but who choose not to become party to the change strategy. Advocacy can address the need for change in policy and/or law as these might become necessary to support and maintain the change being sought. Those who organize advocacy resources to support a prevention strategy need to be knowledgeable about the politics of the situation being addressed in order to use those resources effectively.

Technical assistance supports the development of the technical know-how needed to effect the desired change. Required technical skills may already be in the possession of some key allies within a group undertaking a community development project. These people, in turn, can impart their skills to others within the support system. Technical assistance will be needed throughout the prevention initiative as those involved push toward higher levels of accomplishment.

People who have special insight into the conditions to be changed may also be listed as among the advocates and technical assistance providers. It is important to assure that this group also includes those who experience the problem that is of concern. Too often such persons are relegated to a "client" status and are not respected as resource people who have a unique vantage point. They can be valuable consultants to other key allies who are not directly experiencing the conditions to be changed.

A key dynamic in this approach to prevention is related to the identification and engagement in the key allies group of those who can control or influence various aspects of the conditions that need to be changed. Again, these people may also be included in one or more of the other three groups.

Consider the following example:

A Community Development Workshop is organized, and the first part of the Youth Opportunity Planning Process (YOPP) identifies certain conditions existing in the public schools of the city as one of the more important contributors to the problems young people are having. The results of Part II of the YOPP reveal that the workshop participants believe this factor is basically situational in nature and beyond the control of individual students, that it can best be approached by changing adult behavior, that it calls for preventive strategies that need to be focused upon changing specific conditions. Further, the group does not believe that this factor is being approached at present in a planned and systematic manner. Through using the framework provided by Part III of the YOPP, and with the help of the Prevention Formula, the group begins to develop a prevention strategy. They describe Condition A and Condition B to their satisfaction.

When they list people who can exercise some control over Condition A, they find themselves listing school administrators, policy board members, teachers, students and parents. Each of these groups is represented among the workshop participants. When they identify needed resource people, they again list these groups, which include themselves. As they consider the behavior changes that will be needed, they find they are talking about their own behavior. As they identify key allies, both those who can be counted upon and those capable of blocking the path to Condition B, they are identifying their own peers. They recognize, too, that they have within the group of workshop participants both advocacy and technical assistance resources that can contribute significantly to the desired change. This awareness sheds a new kind of light on the situation which challenges the group to a commitment to act upon it.

Advocacy and technical assistance — twin forces for positive change — are essential ingredients in the support system needed for prevention. As with all aspects of an effective prevention effort, they can be systematically developed, organized and made useful if those involved are aware of their importance and potential contribution.

In summary, advocacy focuses upon *what might be* while technical assistance focuses upon *how to do it.* Because the technology for bringing about positive change exists, advocacy of prevention without making use of technical assistance may border on being irresponsible. It is not hard to convince people, *in principle,* that prevention is highly desirable. Helping people to implement prevention strategies and to deal with the political and economic factors which are involved is the realm of technical assistance. The availability of effective technical assistance which enables people to plan their strategy and realize its goals is quite often the missing ingredient in making effective prevention a reality.

DEVELOPING LOCAL AND STATEWIDE PREVENTION NETWORKS

In his discussion of the trend from hierarchies to networking, John Naisbitt says "the failure of hierarchies to solve society's problems forced people to talk to one another — and that was the beginning of networks."[19] Naisbitt describes this growing phenomenon by saying, "Simply stated, networks are people talking to each other, sharing ideas, information and resources."

Anne W. Dosher, who has for a number of years been training people in the strategies of networking for improving human services, defines networking as "the intentional use of personal skills and relationships in order to identify, develop and negotiate the exchange of resources within newly articulated and defined fields of activity which share a common purpose."

In the writer's experience with building support systems for prevention, some of the most exciting examples of networking have involved people who work within large state-level bureaucracies cooperating across bureaucratic lines with others from state and local public and private organizations. Networks also have broken down barriers between young people and adults and between professional and non-professional persons interested in positive youth development. Alliances have been built between elected officials, administrative decision makers, service providers and other community people.

The positive thrust of prevention has a way of encouraging people to work together in a cooperative manner. A basic notion that is becoming increasingly clear to an expanding number of people is that *prevention concepts are generic in nature*. The definition of prevention suggested in this book and the concepts and strategies that make that definition operational can be applied to a wide variety of concerns. The definition is "wellness-oriented" in that it focuses on creating conditions that promote the well-being of people. This can be directed toward child abuse as well as delinquency, toward emotional disturbance as well as learning problems, or toward drug and alcohol abuse as well as family breakdown. This reality is important for local policy development because it means that *local and statewide prevention networks can promote capacity for confronting any and all of these social ills*. It means that the predominant pattern within which concerns about these and other urgent matters are pursued in a fragmented, wastefully competitive and essentially ineffective manner must be changed if prevention is to be given the emphasis it deserves.

The fact that this fragmented pattern is forced upon communities by state and national policy and funding guidelines in both the public and private voluntary sectors gives the local community no excuse, for that pattern has been adopted and supported vigorously at the local level as well. Those who challenge it quickly learn that they are faced with powerful forces of vested interests that resist change effectively.

Those who would foster the building of a local prevention network, then, have a clear task if they are to make much headway. They do have a forceful kind of logic on their side. This logic says that (a) what is happening now is not working well, (b) there is a definition of prevention that can be embraced by people from many functional areas, (c) the skills and strategies which flow from that definition can be applied to many kinds of social problems, (d) those skills and strategies can be easily taught to expanding numbers of people and (e) the management and application of prevention methods can be designed and implemented at no or little additional cost through using the existing professional and voluntary human resources of the community. All of this can be pursued and accomplished within the existing purposes and missions of the various governmental units and human service and civic organizations of the community, though it will require changes in organizational goals and objectives. What this means, then, is that the kind of change that is needed to support an emphasis on prevention is basically a change toward understanding the nature of prevention and redeploying resources in that direction. This necessarily means new learning, new thinking and new behaving on the part of many people. Though it may seem so, this, in reality, is not such a radical change.

A shift toward prevention is not a radical change because the basic values of most communities, their units of government and their human service systems are essentially those stated in the Service Mode in Chapter III. Adoption of these values creates a prevention network as a natural, even inevitable, part of the community's efforts to achieve continuing community improvement. Those who would work toward a prevention network have a good basis for beginning. Those who would resist it, especially those who are in positions of public trust and leadership, may be persuaded to give the matter their careful consideration through the use of positive, well organized and forceful advocacy that is backed up by practical and readily available technical assistance.

The building of a local network to support prevention is best approached through a developmental process. That is, it is best to build from the ground up, beginning with the natural resources of the community. Three or four people with a clear purpose and well developed objectives can initiate the process. The building blocks of a local network need to be placed carefully and at a pace that is appropriate for the community. At each stage along the way key allies are needed to support and pursue the specific steps that are designed. Many of the tools that are needed have been described in this book; many others can be added.

Building a support system for prevention is a natural and logical part of the prevention process itself. A simple example serves as an illustration.

A Community Development Workshop was attended by a group of 30 people selected for their interest in youth development. On the first day of the workshop the group indentified three factors to which they would give their attention for further planning and action. These were (1) poor communication and negative influence within the family, (2) concern about schools not providing adequate learning experiences for students and (3) the lack of meaningful leisure time activities to which young people have access. There was general agreement that these factors were not getting adequate attention in a planned and systematic manner in the community.

During the second day of the workshop the participants divided themselves into three groups, with one focused on each of the three factors. Each group organized itself to continue working on its factor for the next three months. The purpose of each of these task groups was to develop an action plan during that time.

Each group included young people, an elected official, three human service professionals and some business people. Most of the adults also were parents. It was agreed that the human service professionals would negotiate with their organizations for permission for each of them to spend 10% of their work time serving as staff support to a task group during the three-month period and for secretarial help to be provided. This plan not only would contribute to interagency communication, but also would provide a staff team for each task group. The plan was readily accepted by each organization because the focus of the task groups was clearly within their organizational missions. In fact, they saw it as an opportunity to pursue some of their own objectives. In addition, it gave these organizations some good publicity in the community. To have been uncooperative would have been highly questionable for them.

Having three professionals on each task group meant that each group had 144 staff hours available to it over the three months. Careful planning made it possible to reach numerous other people. Methods were informal and low keyed. Each group collected extensive information about its problem area while generating considerable interest about it in the community.

At the end of the three months, as a natural result of this focused activity, each task group had identified numerous key allies, had become well informed about its area of focus and the resources in the community related to it, had developed an action plan to be pursued for the remainder of the year and had, in fact, created a network of resource people who were available to help carry out the action plan.

This example illustrates several important elements of a community development approach to prevention. It is a very positive experience, it can give structure and direction to people's energy, it can fit readily into the ongoing work of the human service organizations of the community, it is an experience in community education, and, if the action plans are well designed, it can have specific impact on arenas of community life that vitally affect people.

Once an experience like this has occurred, there is a group of people who have gained on-the-job training in designing and implementing prevention strategies. This new skill can then be applied to any aspect of the community. *In the process, a support network has been created.* Without some kind of supportive network there is little way that the collective and cumulative experience of the community can become the basis of growth and development.

The emphasis in this discussion of networking has been on building from the ground up within the local community. Since prevention is essentially a local responsibility that focuses upon local conditions and engages local resources, it is important to assure that this kind of local focus is maintained throughout the process. There are, however, some useful ways that support for local prevention initiatives can be generated at the state level and beyond. Many local resource organizations are affiliated with statewide or national structures. This immediately presents some potential problems that it is well to consider at the earliest stages. *State and national level resources must be in a support role if the emphasis is to be on developing local capacity.* It is not unusual for persons at the state and national levels, which are removed from the community, to see themselves as being in the "driver's seat" in relation to prevention. The result has often been wasteful, misleading and generally unproductive.

Several tendencies might complicate the nature of the relationship between the local community and the state and national levels. Initiatives for prevention coming from the state or national levels may enter the local community as prescribed structures which inhibit or severely limit a developmental, community-based approach. State or national initiative may take place from within the framework of categorical programs designed at the state or national level, fragmenting the effort from the beginning and reducing the potential for networking. State agencies will at times hire staff people as state employees and place them in the local community to initiate prevention activity. When this happens, accountability must be to the state agency and this can cause confusion. Local people are often forced into the position of deferring to the presumed expertise of the outsider rather than finding the state or national level person or agency supportive of their own efforts. Technical resource people at the state and national levels frequently lack the skills and knowledge related to prevention concepts and strategies that are necessary to assist local communities.

When funding is involved, the relationship between the local and the state or national levels becomes even more complicated because the person from outside the community assumes a monitoring role. The support role that might be carried by the outsider tends to be subordinated to a concern about whether or not the funds are being managed in accordance with the funding body's expectations. Whatever potential there may have been for useful technical assistance is often lost.

What is an appropriate role for the state or national agency or resource person in a local prevention effort? Is there a way the relationship can be defined, negotiated and understood so it is realistically supportive of prevention? The concepts, values and assumptions suggested earlier point toward several useful ideas for shaping roles and responsibilities at the state and national levels.

Criteria for Shaping State and National Level Roles and Responsibilities to Support Local Prevention Efforts

1. The basic responsibility for identifying the focus and designing the strategy for prevention belongs to the local community.

2. Resources at the state and national levels can support and assist in building local prevention capacity through providing technical services such as training, evaluation assistance and consultation, with community involvement in determining how they can best be used.

3. In some limited and carefully planned ways, state and federal funding can be supportive to local community prevention efforts. (Caution should be used in this matter. In relation to prevention, funding can be more distracting than it is enabling.)

4. Personnel who work at state and national levels should have sound technical skills in order to offer credible services at the local level.

After a clear understanding of the nature and use of state and national resources for supporting local prevention efforts is established, it becomes possible to begin to build local and statewide networks for prevention. There are several strategic reasons for organizing at the state level. First, state law, state agencies and the locally based offices of state agencies can all affect the local prevention effort positively or negatively, and it is important to make sure this happens in a positive way. Second, advocacy coalitions from a number of local networks, if they work in concert, can help to shape state law and the way state agencies relate to the local community. Third, as local and state level capacity is developed, valuable technical assistance can be offered among and between the local and state level resources. (Frequently the state is in need of the technical assistance that can be offered by people from the local level.) Fourth, a statewide network can sponsor useful events that can bring in stimuli from outside the state and organize the in-state resources to good advantage. Fifth, as a number of communities become organized locally and work with state agencies, they can collectively deal with the national level from a stronger position. The statewide network, then, is understood completely in relation to the utility it can have for supporting local prevention efforts.

In a northeastern state, staff people from a large number of local prevention projects formed a statewide coalition. In their dealings with the state youth agency they were able to encourage the establishment of a state-level position through which they could coordinate local and state planning and action. For several years they pursued a productive working relationship. Strong initiatives were taken in the areas of legislation, coordination of statewide activity, training, technical assistance for the state and local communities, the formation of a statewide technical assistance team and the allocation of state funds which were matched by local funds for local prevention activity.

In a midwestern state several people at the state level took some interesting initiatives. They searched through the state statutes related to several large state agencies (education, corrections, labor, social services, etc.) and found that all of these agencies had mandates to be active in relation to prevention. They contacted people in each agency and discovered that there were no working definitions of the word prevention, there was very little in the way of organized approaches to carry out these legal mandates, there was no communication among the agencies related to prevention, and there was a general lack of direction within all of the agencies in regard to what they might do, collectively or separately. In these discussions it was agreed that some effort to bring them together to see what might be done in a coordinated manner would be useful.

A planning group was formed and outside consultants were engaged. A statewide workshop was held, bringing together state and local people, including a group of young people. This meeting was positive and productive. A working definition of prevention was agreed upon, and a steering group began to develop a statewide plan to foster prevention planning and activity in a coordinated manner. The emphasis throughout has been on promoting local responsibility for prevention with state-level support. A number of local communities made their bids to become demonstration communities. Each community committed itself to a two-year program with the understanding that it would receive technical assistance from the statewide network for shaping and sustaining its efforts.

Whatever shape it may take, some way that people can begin to have purposive communication and build on their experience is necessary if a prevention emphasis is to make any gains. It is unfortunate when this coordinating activity drains away valuable energy that could be going into local prevention initiatives. That need not happen, for it is possible to work together at the local and state levels in ways that enhance, encourage and support strong local prevention efforts.

THE STATEWIDE POSITIVE YOUTH DEVELOPMENT INITIATIVE

An approach that brings together all of the concepts, strategies, tools and skills that have been presented throughout this book is the statewide Positive Youth Development (PYD) initiative.[20] This new kind of experience is currently under way in several states, and it is uniquely suited for a tight economy in which it is unlikely that new funds will be made available for prevention. The PYD initiative holds much promise for gaining better results from the existing human resources of the community. While the PYD initiative is specifically focused on promoting positive *youth* development, it is a strategy that can be directed toward any of a variety of concerns, such as the specific needs of older citizens or other populations with special needs.

A PYD initiative is defined as a cooperative effort in a number of local communities, with encouragement from a statewide support system, to create conditions which promote the well-being of young people. It is based upon concepts that emphasize the better utilization of existing resources, youth/adult partnerships, and cooperation across functional and organizational lines. It places a high priority on a positive prevention approach, though it recognizes the need for remedial services and resources. Persons skilled in remediation are engaged in the PYD initiative as key allies.

A strong emphasis is placed upon equipping people with skills for positive community change, thereby leaving in place both individual and organizational capacity that can be applied to other pursuits. Assertive community strategies are fostered through action training provided through the Community Development Workshop. Two states, Wisconsin and North Carolina, have well-developed PYD initiatives at the time of this writing. The Wisconsin experience was described in an article entitled "Cooperation on a Statewide Basis," by Dennis M. Maloney. He states in this article published in 1981:

> It has involved turning the negative forces of the times into driving forces and actually utilizing the "no new money" reality as a timely opportunity to bring more valuable resources and public attention to the entire initiative. When agencies and organizations can no longer depend on increased budgets to foster prevention efforts they are forced to make the most of current resources whereby dedicated staff, community volunteers and young people can emerge as leaders of a more solidly founded grassroots prevention strategy.[21]

In 1982, Lisa Brunette and Michael Sullivan, co-chairpersons of the Wisconsin PYD steering committee, made the following observations:

> "We have been utilizing these ideas in Wisconsin communities for three years, and have found them to be effective vehicles for development of collaboration among individuals, organizations and systems to create changes in conditions which cause problems for young people. They are cost-effective in that the major thrust is upon reallocation of existing resources in communities and organizations. They demonstrate that decisions can and should be made at the local level, when local citizens are given the skills and opportunity to identify and analyze causes of problems, and design a plan of action to deal with those causes."

Donald E. Percy, who in 1982 was Secretary of the Wisconsin Department of Health and Social Services, made these additional observations about the Wisconsin effort:

The PYD process is being implemented in 15 communities across the state involving over 1,500 community volunteers. Of particular interest is the fact that we have accomplished this by redeploying staff at the state level who have extensive experience in remedial services to contribute a portion of their work week to this prevention initiative. These state staff in turn are enjoined with local people in a truly community based effort. Our goal is to develop a viable continuum of service from prevention to effective and least restrictive intervention. In Wisconsin as in many other states, we are faced with the task of maintaining this initiative without new federal dollars. Thus this reallocation of resources allows us to create and implement these new ideas within times of cutting back. It is our feeling that what is really needed during these uncertain times is a commitment to take charge and be innovative with our limited resources and in the process foster viable solutions to difficult problems.

Kenneth Foster of the North Carolina Division of Youth Services states that "No idea in my recent memory has stirred more excitement or generated more interagency cooperation in North Carolina than has the PYD initiative. In a time of dwindling resources, PYD offers the opportunity to make a positive impact on a wide variety of juvenile justice issues."

There is a strong rationale for demonstrating the effectiveness of a statewide PYD initiative. Some of the more compelling considerations are:

1. A strong emphasis on a concept of prevention that can get positive results in the home, school, neighborhood and the larger community is always needed, but especially when more expensive remedial programs are being cut back.

2. The collective experience of a number of communities, observed and documented on a statewide basis, can add to the overall knowledge of effective approaches and strategies for promoting positive change.

3. Dissemination of information gained through this experience encourages communities to be creative by giving them positive visibility across the state. This can create a statewide atmosphere for taking new risks in the direction of positive change.

4. The PYD initiative provides an excellent opportunity for young people to carry responsible roles while working with adults to promote positive community change. This enriches the experience of both the young people and the adults and increases the probability for approaches that are acceptable to the young people of the community.

5. Rather than arousing a negative response from organizations which offer remedial services, the approach uses their experience as a resource for assessing community conditions and designing strategies that will attain prevention goals.

6. The PYD initiative can have positive impact on the policy, management and service delivery domains at the local and state levels. The training used addresses issues in each of these domains and engages people in them in experiential approaches to reexamining their practices and attitudes.

7. The concepts, strategies, tools and skills that are used can be applied to any community. They are workable in different cultures and in cross-cultural situations, as well as in both rural and urban settings. It has this flexibility because process rather than prescriptive methods are used.

8. The methods used have brought people from mental health, juvenile justice, education, drug and alcohol abuse, recreation and other fields into cooperative relationships. The response has been positive because people have recognized that the conditions which produce the symptoms with which each of these functional areas is concerned are caused or promoted by common factors.

The methods used in Wisconsin and North Carolina have demonstrated some new directions which deserve additional testing and refinement. The seven elements described below build on the experience of those two states and include some additional ideas which can help to create an effective statewide support system to local communities.

These elements are designed to (a) build upon existing local and state level strength and capacity, (b) make use of existing networks and other resources, (c) encourage and support the development of new networks locally and statewide, and (d) leave new capacity in place that can be used in other pursuits.

The Statewide Steering Committee

An early task is to organize a statewide steering committee made up of young people and adults who represent communities and organizations at the state and local levels. This group provides the leadership and helps to shape the initiative as it develops statewide. As leaders of the PYD initiative, it is important that members of this group maintain a high level of interest, commitment and motivation. This group will probably need training to assist its members in developing their leadership skills.

The Statewide Technical Assistance Team

A team of people who will serve as technical assistance providers learn the basic methods of the program, which they add to their own skills and methods. They are deployed in a planned and systematic manner to the various tasks related to the elements described below.

This group needs to be equipped with a sound conceptual base, the needed training skills, consultative skills and knowledge of how local communities can undertake prevention initiatives. Basic training is provided to assure that all members of the technical assistance team can work effectively with local community groups.

This team is organized into sub-groups which can work in various areas of the state.

Regional and Local PYD Orientation Sessions

People around the state are given an orientation to PYD concepts and strategies through brief regional and local meetings that are sponsored by local groups. These may include human service networks, city councils and county supervisors, civic clubs, churches or coalitions of interested people and organizations. These sessions occur early in the life of the initiative to give people an opportunity to determine their interest in undertaking a local PYD initiative. If they so choose, the resources of the technical assistance team can be available to assist them. The next three elements can then follow in sequence.

It is useful to require a commitment from communities selected as demonstration communities. This commitment is for a period of time during which the local group will pursue the three stages of a prevention initiative described in Chapter II. This will encourage the community group to persist with full knowledge of what is involved. A commitment also is made to the community that needed technical assistance will be available to them throughout this period. In Wisconsin a two-year commitment was made by each community.

Technical Assistance to Local Steering Committees

The quality of leadership in the local community is a key to the success of a local PYD initiative. An objective, then, of the statewide effort is to promote the development of local leadership so the effort can gain needed momentum. Being sensitive to the amount of technical assistance needed to support the local leadership is critically important. Experience has shown that this support is needed at all stages as the local group goes through the process of tackling its first priority area. Success generates more interest and a willingness to deal with more challenging matters in the community.

The initial planning by the local steering committee sets the stage for other steps to be taken. Helping this group get an early sense of direction and understanding of the potential of a PYD initiative will assist the local effort to get under way on a sound basis.

Community Development Training in Local Communities

A key event in the local PYD initiative is the Community Development Workshop which trains local people for the task. This training event is part of a sequence of activities that give structure to the local initiative. Participants in the process give it content. The Community Development Workshop, as has been described, focuses on concepts, strategies, tools and skills for prevention. It assists the participants in viewing their community from a prevention perspective and engages them in planning for action. The length and format for the workshop should be designed with the local steering committee and will depend upon the preferences and convenience of those who attend. It can be offered as a weekend retreat, during the regular work week, or on a basis of several hours per week over several weeks, if trainers from the technical assistance team can be available.

The success of a Community Development Workshop as part of a community action plan depends, in large measure, upon the quality of planning and follow-up. The workshop should not be seen as an isolated activity or an end in itself. It is part of a well-planned strategy for community change. It helps to prepare people to participate in the PYD initiative, but it is also a method for promoting change in the community. It brings together a group of people who do not usually work together (young people, adult citizens, human service providers and decision makers). In this sense it introduces a new dimension to the community's efforts to promote positive youth development.

The Community Prevention Inventory

The Community Prevention Inventory presented at the end of Chapter III can be a useful tool in the sequence of events related to the Community Development Workshop. If the information it suggests is generated prior to the workshop, the results can be presented during the workshop. Alternatively, the inventory can be used as part of the workshop follow-up strategy. It will give participants in the process a clear sense of the place of prevention in the community and will help to clarify directions for future action.

Publication of Regular Newsletters

Communication on a statewide basis is essential in a PYD initiative, and the documentation of various aspects of the initiative through a circulated publication will encourage more assertive approaches at the local and statewide levels. Conceptual stimulation, strategy ideas, case studies and other information about what is going on in relation to the PYD initiative can promote increased interest and goal-directed action.

This publication can be a newsletter distributed to city councils, county boards of supervisors, tribal councils, school boards, state legislators and other decision making groups; youth serving organizations of all kinds; youth-run organizations; churches and interested citizens.

It may be possible for the statewide steering committee to get assistance from a large business or corporation which has typesetting and printing equipment to produce the newsletter.

Information about PYD initiatives in other states can also be useful for the stimulation of new ideas. The exchange of newsletters between and among states provides encouragement for all. (The Wisconsin newsletter is called the *PYD Link,* and the North Carolina newsletter is called the *PYD Piper.*)

* * *

A PYD initiative is an assertive, goal-oriented undertaking, and it is important that documentation and evaluation of the experience is built into the effort. The planning models used in the Community Development Workshop include evaluation. Participants should be encouraged to develop clear indicators that will tell them to what extent they have moved from their current situation toward the outcomes they wish to achieve. Process description is important to capture the experience of the program in an anecdotal fashion, and outcome measures can be developed with careful action planning. Encouraging people at the local and state levels to consider the importance of evaluation and build it into their efforts is an essential part of a PYD initiative.

The opportunity for participation in a PYD initiative is open-ended. The initiative potentially involves anyone interested in promoting the well-being of young people, but the strategies to be fostered specifically focus on the participation of selected decision makers, human service professionals, young people and adult citizens (parents, business people, etc.). The youth participation component can work through existing youth organizations, but it should actively seek to include young people who are not a part of such groups. Young people who have been identified as delinquent or characterized by some other type of negative label can and should be included as potentially valuable resource people.

The level of participation in a PYD initiative broadens as people respond to the positive invitation to become involved. The selection of demonstration communities for the first year of a PYD initiative is a useful approach. This enables the resources of the statewide technical assistance team to be used wisely and not spread too thin. While people from these selected communities become involved in the initiative, they and many others will become exposed to the concepts and have an opportunity to apply them at the individual, organizational and community levels as a result of this exposure.

THE CHALLENGE OF BEING PROACTIVE IN A REACTIVE WORLD

Strange as it may seem, an attempt to encourage an interest in prevention immediately attracts a variety of reactive forces that may appear as formidable obstacles. Those forces are at work in the thought processes of individuals, in families, in organizations of all kinds, in governmental bodies, in institutions. Entire professions become enmeshed in the reactive mindset.

A positive approach to prevention must compete with long-standing commitments that have been made to personal, organizational, professional and institutional behavior patterns. The *status quo* is always protected by behavior, individual and collective. The conditions underlying the numerous symptoms for which elaborate remedial responses have been devised are perpetuated by behavior, and the corrective systems which have been designed often appear to be locked into the reactive mode. Political and economic structures and all of the personal and organizational vested interests that sustain them support the maintenance of reactive commitments.

In short, we live in an essentially reactive world. Those who would dare to promote change soon discover in many different ways just how strong the maintenance forces are. It is not surprising that many people give in to these forces and make conscious decisions not to "fight the system." When this kind of deference occurs within the benevolent organizations and institutions of our communities, there exists an incongruity that is at once obvious and perplexing. We see it among clergy who work within rigid ecclesiastical bureaucracies. We see it among educators within schools that defy change. It is apparent in local and state-level human service bureaucracies. It is as if the people who manage and work in these organizations are not in charge but are controlled by *the pattern.*

And yet, change is going on all around us – change that is being fostered by people who have a sense of direction and the necessary instincts, if not specific skills, for making the change happen. Everyone possesses some of these intuitive strengths, and we are challenged to work together to put the key in the lock that can open ourselves, our peers, our organizations and our institutions to more positive approaches.

The challenge of becoming proactive in a reactive world is an exciting one, indeed. Those who are attuned to the positive emphasis, the new venture that will make things different, the opportunity to create the new condition that will benefit people – these people are continually finding others engaged in similar endeavors. Many of them are ready to join forces with other like-minded people. Some are looking for allies and support from others. Still others are ready to follow the lead of those who have a clearer sense of direction.

If the world tends to resist those who will run the risks of pursuing the kind of positive approach to prevention that has been presented, it is not hostile toward them. The potential of our experiencing a significant paradigm shift toward a more balanced approach to human services and community betterment is quite promising. Preparing ourselves for the task and encouraging others to join the venture is enticing to enough people today to give hope.

ACHIEVING A BALANCE IN HUMAN SERVICE RESOURCES

Discovering the meaning of prevention leads to a more balanced approach to using the resources of our communities. In Chapter I, the see-saw cartoon suggests that human service systems are far out of balance because of the emphasis that is placed on remedial methods. It is the writer's belief that we do not need to take away from remedial resources to bring the system more into balance. Rather, prevention will take its rightful place in human service endeavors when it is presented in a positive manner that demonstrates clearly how it can enrich all aspects of community life, including human service systems.

Achieving a balance in human service resources does not necessarily mean that equal funding will be given to all four quadrants of human service activity. That is probably not needed. The fact of the matter is that it does cost more to keep a person in prison, in a mental institution or in some other custodial environment than to work in the community on the conditions which led to the placement. It does cost more to counsel or provide therapy to individuals than to organize groups of people to change community conditions. The financial burdens of remediation will always cost more than work in the prevention quadrants.

Achieving a balance in human service resources is directly related to changes in attitudes and commitments. It does not set up a competitive struggle between prevention and remediation. Rather, it focuses on providing a new paradigm which demonstrates clearly that prevention is everyone's business, including those who are skilled in remedial work and have committed themselves to it. Indeed, as has been strongly emphasized, those who work in Quadrant 4 need to be engaged as key allies in prevention initiatives.

Achieving a balance in human service resources involves discovering that a positive approach to prevention enriches any and all efforts to bring about change in the community. It brings people from all parts of the community into cooperative approaches to improving community conditions. It builds new alliances, opens the possibility for new relationships and unites as colleagues people who otherwise would not have known one another. It uses the technologies for change that have been developed in many disciplines and work places. It channels human energy into productive strategies that are focused on carefully selected goals.

In Chapter I a list of six "Characteristics of Effective Prevention Strategies" was presented to show how these qualities differ from some common attitudes about prevention. It is useful to list these again at the end of the book to give the reader an opportunity to assess his or her own understanding of prevention.

CHARACTERISTICS OF EFFECTIVE PREVENTION STRATEGIES

1. Prevention is realistic and goal oriented.
2. Prevention is practical and specific.
3. Prevention is designed to attain measurable results.
4. Prevention is focused upon short and long range impact.
5. Prevention is cost effective and cost reducing.
6. Prevention is not just a luxury, but a necessity if a balanced community approach to human development is to be achieved.

If this book can assist people in acquiring an understanding of prevention that moves closer to the qualities outlined in these six statements, and if it encourages them to commit some of their energy and resources to applying that understanding, in cooperation with others, to specific tasks of community betterment, it will have achieved its intended purposes.

Beyond that, we will all gain if we can vigorously reexamine our purposes and goals at many levels – personally, organizationally, collectively as a community, state and nation – and ask how we can actively create conditions which promote the well-being of people. If we do that seriously and with a clear understanding that what we do can make a real difference in those conditions, we will probably find that we begin to use our many resources in different and more positive ways.

Discovering the meaning of prevention is a transformative process. It gives us a new understanding of what is happening around us. It can renew and redirect our personal lives in more positive directions. It can renew and redirect the organizations within which we work. It can revitalize our families and create new levels of relating and understanding within them. It can, if we apply ourselves to the task, help to make our communities more livable, more humane, more just and more caring places in which to live.

These incredibly positive expectations are not related to any panacea or utopian dream. They are, rather, based upon a belief that people can become responsible, within realistic limits, for shaping the conditions under which they live, work, learn, use their leisure and otherwise spend their time. They are based, further, on the knowledge that people working together can determine what they want their communities to become and move increasingly toward that goal. Equipping ourselves with the concepts, strategies, tools and skills for the task is a major step. Building a support system to expand and sustain our efforts is another. Realizing that our efforts do make a difference can then encourage us to take on more difficult challenges. In this way the discovery becomes real, the rewards become tangible, the balance is achieved, and prevention will assume its rightful place in our values, actions and the use of our energy and resources. □

FOOTNOTES

1. *Webster's Seventh New Collegiate Dictionary* (Springfield, MA: G. and C. Merriam Company, 1972), p. 674.

2. Robert R. Blake and Jane S. Mouton, *Consultation* (Reading, MA: Addison-Wesley Publishing Co., 1976).

3. George S. Odiorne, *Management and the Activity Trap* (New York: Harper and Row, 1974).

4. *Webster's Seventh New Collegiate Dictionary, op. cit.,* p. 656.

5. David A. Bundy, "Common Sense in New Hampshire: The Manchester Youth Policy," *NEW DESIGNS for Youth Development,* vol. 2 (January/February, 1981), p. 13.

6. Gordon L. Lippitt, *Visualizing Change: Model Building and the Change Process* (San Diego: University Associates, Inc., 1973).

7. William A. Lofquist, "The Prevention Formula," *The Arizona Technical Assistance Review,* vol. 1, (March/April, 1978), pp. 4-6.

8. Kurt Lewin, "Quasi-stationary Social Equilibria and the Problem of Permanent Change," *The Planning of Change,* W.G. Bennis, K.D. Benne, and R. Chin (eds.) (New York: Holt, Rinehart and Winston, 1961), pp. 235-238.

9. Useful discussion of force field analysis is found in the following books: Morris S. Speir, "Kurt Lewin's 'Force Field Analysis'," *The 1973 Annual Handbook for Group Facilitators,* John E. Jones and J. William Pfeiffer (eds.) (San Diego: University Associates, Inc., 1973) pp. 111-113; Walton C. Boshear and Karl G. Albrecht, *Understanding People: Models and Concepts* (San Diego: University Associates, Inc., 1977), pp. 208-211; Gordon L. Lippitt, *op. cit.,* pp. 172-173, 205-207, 308-309, 314-331; Dorothy P. Craig, *Hip Pocket Guide to Planning and Evaluation* (Austin, TX: Learning Concepts, 1978), pp. 40-45.

10. David H. Jenkins, "Force Field Analysis Applied to a School Situation," *The Planning of Change,* W.G. Bennis, K.D. Benne, and R. Chin (eds.) (New York: Holt, Rinehart and Winston, 1961), pp. 238-244.

11. Robert F. Mager, *Developing Attitude Toward Learning* (Belmont, CA: Fearon Publishers, Inc., 1968.), p. 69.

12. Thomas D. Bird, "So Who's Interested in Results? A Skeptic's View of Evaluation of Youth Services," *NEW DESIGNS for Youth Development,* vol. 1, (July/August, 1980), pp. 19-24.

13. John Van Maanen, "The Process of Program Evaluation," *The Grantsmanship Center News,* vol. 5, (January/February, 1979), p. 30.

14. Marilyn Ferguson, *The Aquarian Conspiracy, Personal and Social Transformation in the 1980s* (Los Angeles: J.P. Tarcher, Inc., 1980).

15. John Naisbitt, *Megatrends: Ten New Directions Transforming Our Lives* (New York: Warner Books, 1982).

16. Ferguson, *op. cit.,* pp. 27-28.

17. *The Random House Dictionary of the English Language: The Unabridged Edition* (New York: Random House, 1967), p. 22.

18. *Ibid.*

19. Naisbitt, *op. cit.,* p. 191.

20. William A. Lofquist, "The Statewide Positive Youth Development Initiative: A Strategy for Today's Economy," *NEW DESIGNS for Youth Development,* vol. 3 (March/April, 1982), pp. 24-29.

21. Dennis M. Maloney, "Cooperation on a Statewide Basis," *NEW DESIGNS for Youth Development,* vol. 2, (March/April, 1981), p. 23.

ANNOTATED BIBLIOGRAPHY

Allen, Robert F. *Beat the System: A Way to Create More Human Environments.* New York: McGraw-Hill Book Company, 1980.

Provides a way of understanding the "culture" of an organization or community and a strategy for changing those aspects of the culture that need changing. Several case studies illustrate the process. A positive approach for building "success environments" is both practical and optimistic.

Bennis, Warren G., Kenneth D. Benne, and Robert Chin (eds.) *The Planning of Change: Readings in the Applied Behavioral Sciences.* New York: Holt, Rinehart and Winston, 1961.

A book of readings, both classic and modern, on the roots of planned change, conceptual tools for the change agent (social systems and change models), the dynamics of the influence process, and programs and technologies of planned change. An excellent reference work.

Blake, Robert R. and Jane S. Mouton. *Consultation.* Reading, MA: Addison-Wesley Publishing Company, 1976.

A three-dimensional model called the "consulcube" provides a framework for looking at the focal issues, kinds of intervention and units of change that are related to the consultative process. Broad in scope and rich in illustration.

Boshear, Walton C. and Karl G. Albrecht. Understanding People: Models and Concepts. San Diego: University Associates, Inc., 1977.

A wide range of concepts and models that focus on interpersonal and organizational situations. Well organized and practical for use in team building, staff development and other training settings.

Craig, Dorothy P. *Hip Pocket Guide to Planning and Evaluation.* Austin, TX: Learning Concepts, 1978.

A practical, step-by-step approach, with easy-to-use worksheets for each part of the process of planning and evaluating a project. The user is encouraged to build in the capacity for evaluation from the beginning of the planning process.

Davis, Larry Nolan and Earl McCallon. *Planning, Conducting and Evaluating Workshops.* Austin, TX: Learning Concepts, 1974.

Covers all aspects of shaping, delivering and assessing the training process. Very readable.

Ferguson, Marilyn. *The Aquarian Conspiracy: Personal and Social Transformation in the 1980s.* Los Angeles: J.P. Tarcher, Inc., 1980.

A provocative, wide-ranging book about changing aspects of our personal and social experience. Considers the various "paradigm shifts" that are taking place and how these are being fostered by assertive people who promote transformation in their own lives and the institutions of the community.

Fessler, Donald R. *Facilitating Community Change: A Basic Guide.* San Diego: University Associates, Inc., 1976.

Provides an overview of a variety of matters to be considered in promoting community change, and includes many references for more detailed information.

Harvey, Donald F. and Donald R. Brown, *An Experiential Approach to Organization Development.* Englewood Cliffs, NJ: Prentice-Hall, Inc., 1976.

Includes a comprehensive set of concepts and structured workshop activities which enable participants to explore various aspects of organizational change. Useful both for the adaptable activities and the insight provided into different elements of change strategies.

Jones, John E. and J. William Pfeiffer (eds.). *The Annual Handbook for Group Facilitators.* San Diego: University Associates, Inc., 1972 to the present (annual volumes).

Each of these volumes presents structured experiences, instruments, lecturettes on important concepts, theory and practice considerations, and resources related to individual, group, organizational and community change. A valuable collection that is easy to use.

Lippitt, Gordon L. *Visualizing Change: Model Building and the Change Process.* San Diego: University Associates, Inc., 1973.

A thorough discussion of the design and use of change models. Considers models for human resource development, individual change, group change and organizational change.

_____ and Ronald Lippitt. *The Consulting Process in Action.* San Diego: University Associates, Inc., 1978.

Presents consultation as a two-way, collaborative process. Examines various consultant roles, strategies and skills. A useful guide for developing consultative skills.

Naisbitt, John. *Megatrends: Ten New Directions Transforming Our Lives.* New York: Warner Books, 1982.

A dynamic examination of ten important trends the author sees as operating in our national life. These trends have many implications for local, state and national level efforts to promote positive change.

NEW DESIGNS for Youth Development. Tucson, AZ: Associates for Youth Development, Inc., published bi-monthly.

This publication includes articles which describe various aspects of prevention concepts, strategies, and program examples.

Odiorne, George S. *Management and the Activity Trap.* New York: Harper and Row, Publishers, 1974.

This book describes a common phenomenon, the activity trap, and discusses "how to avoid it and how to get out of it." A useful concept for helping organizations of all kinds to focus their energies and resources on the attainment of objectives.

_____. *MBO II: A System of Managerial Leadership for the 80s.* Belmont, CA: Fearon Pitman Publishers, 1979.

Presents the philosophy and practice of "management by objectives." Useful for leaders, managers and participants in organizations which have the attainment of results as their purpose.

Schindler-Rainman, Eva and Ronald Lippitt. *The Volunteer Community: Creative Use of Human Resources.* 2d ed. Fairfax, VA: NTL Learning Resources Corporation, 1975.

Includes a useful discussion of voluntarism, its history and present status, and practical guides on the recruitment, orientation, training of volunteers and management of volunteer programs.

_____. *Building the Collaborative Community: Mobilizing Citizens for Action.* Riverside, CA: University of California Extension, 1980.

A practical guide for planning and implementing community action programs which engage citizens. Filled with change models and illustrations of their use.

Other Resources from
Associates for Youth Development, Inc.

THE TECHNOLOGY OF PREVENTION WORKBOOK
A Leadership Development Program
Resource Guide for Workshop Participants
By William A. Lofquist

NEW DESIGNS for Youth Development

A quarterly magazine for people
in the forefront of youth development work!

• National in scope • Futuristic in emphasis
• Prevention in orientation • Practical in application

The Youth Opportunity Planning Process
A Systematic Approach to Involving Community
Groups in Strategic Planning

For additional information contact:
Associates for Youth Development, Inc.
P. O. Box 36748,
Tucson, Arizona 85740
Telephone: (602) 297-1056